# Praise for *Media Fasting*

"Sister Nancy Usselmann's book is well-crafted and timely—it would be difficult to think of a timelier book for her audience, young adults living in the digital world. The stakes are high, and this book adapts a classic Christian spiritual practice to an urgent need for greater freedom in the use of digital means. I willingly recommend it. If you read and put this book into practice, you will love the results."

— Father Timothy Gallagher, OMV, author *of The Discernment of Spirits: An Ignatian Guide to Everyday Living*

"We were made for fullness of life. Jesus came that we might have life to the full. But in the clamoring demands of our media-saturated reality, we often settle for chains of distraction, addiction, and derealization in ourselves, our relationships, and our prayer. *Media Fasting* proposes a practical and spiritually aware approach to breaking chains within our media engagement, emancipating our minds, wills, and hearts to live in the freedom, purpose, and abundance of life with Christ."

— Sister Orianne Pietra René Dyck, FSP, social media manager and media missionary

"In a world filled with noise, it can be challenging to be still and allow God to truly speak to our hearts. Journey with Sister

Nancy Usselmann through a media fast as she invites each of us to be more intentional with the time God has entrusted to us. After six weeks, I believe you will encounter a peace that only Jesus could give."

— David Patterson, host and founder of *Yes Catholic*

"Sister Nancy Usselmann is a seasoned media apostle whose step-by-step practical guide is a gift to anyone seeking to integrate faith and media experiences in daily life. In these pages the reader is invited to journey through a six-week media fast that can lead to a transformed spiritual life. In a digital age marked by many opportunities and challenges in media connectivity, this carefully prepared retreat invites reflection on one's media habits to grow in deeper friendship with Jesus Christ within the community of faith. I am pleased to recommend this hands-on, insightful book wholeheartedly."

— Jem Sullivan, Ph.D., associate professor, School of Theology and Religious Studies, The Catholic University of America

"The people of God today are thirsting for spiritual guidance amid the noises of social media and technology addiction. Sister Nancy's new book serves as a suitable resource for those, both young and old, seeking to redirect their hearts away from the screen and back to the One who offers them everlasting life. Sister Nancy's six-week fast is not only relevant for the modern Church, but necessary for its ongoing purification!"

— Manny Gonzalez, Catholic evangelist and content creator

# MEDIA FASTING

## Six Weeks to Recharge in Christ

by Sister Nancy Usselmann, FSP

Foreword by Jonathan Roumie

**Pauline**
BOOKS & MEDIA
BOSTON

Library of Congress Control Number: 2023951970

ISBN 0-8198-7809-X

ISBN 978-0-8198-7809-0

The Scripture quotations contained herein are from the *New Revised Standard Version Bible: Catholic Edition,* copyright © 1989, 1993, Division of Christian Education of the National Council of the Churches of Christ in the United States of America. Used by permission. All rights reserved.

Cover design by Ryan McQuade

Published by Pauline Books & Media, 50 Saint Pauls Avenue, Boston, MA 02130-3491

Printed in the U.S.A.

www.pauline.org

Pauline Books & Media is the publishing house of the Daughters of St. Paul, an international congregation of women religious serving the Church with the communications media.

1 2 3 4 5 6 7 8 9        30 29 28 27 26 25

For all young adults searching for communion with God
in a digitally hyper-connected world.

And in gratitude for my editors,
Sister Marie Paul Curley, FSP, and Courtney Saponaro,
who brought this book to life and believed in the need
to integrate our life of faith with our media experience.

# Contents

## Part 1

## SPIRITUALLY DRAINED

## Part 2

## SPIRITUAL RECHARGE

# Foreword

IN MY PREVIOUS CAREER as a film and TV location scout in New York City, one of my favorite places to spend time was the Pauline Books and Media store that was once located in Midtown Manhattan next door to a Rand McNally Map shop, an essential repository for all location scouts in the days prior to the ubiquitousness of mobile phone GPS. While preparing to write this foreword, I discovered that, coincidentally, Sister Nancy Usselmann happened to be a manager at that bookstore's location when I would have frequented the shop, though we didn't know each other.

In my times perusing its vast collection of printed books and diverse array of religious items and gifts, the book center always seemed to be this out-of-place sanctuary in the midst of a manic metropolis. Simply stepping inside the store offered an inviting opportunity for a deeper connection to the Divine. It served as a spiritual oasis for me in a concrete desert of a city that often felt like it was too busy and unconcerned to even make room for God, though I eventually realized I simply needed to open my eyes and look a little deeper to see just what gems of spiritual relief my hometown actually offered. I kind of wished I'd spent more time reading and hanging out there than I did. Thankfully, once I moved to Los Angeles years later and got to officially meet and befriend the Daughters of St. Paul, I quickly discovered their West Coast brick-and-mortar bookstore. Same spiritual oasis, different distracted metropolis.

Through my growing fraternity with the sisters—in part due to one of the many side gigs I worked at the time, which brought me into their store routinely—I would continue to find solace and respite there, specifically between the moments I was trying to hustle and muscle my acting career into existence. I have especially cherished my relationship with Sister Nancy, who has become a dear friend, a fellow musical collaborator (for the brief time I spent playing their annual Daughters of St. Paul Christmas Concert), and most importantly, an esteemed prayer warrior whose ministry and care for those in media is unparalleled. I've come to depend on the strength and support of Sister and the Daughters of St. Paul in a very real way, knowing that they have the interests and intentions of those working in the media industry at the core of their mission.

As the trend toward all things digital continues ever forward, the need for an intentional spiritual oasis is more evident than ever. Simply opening our news feed on our devices can provoke a sense of anxiety and overwhelm. We are bombarded with the fear-inducing headlines proliferated by news outlets keen on attracting ever-increasing indexes of eyeballs. Or by the dizzying array of attention-sapping distractions the vortex of social media presents to those seeking sanctuary and peace from the din of the twenty-first century.

The choices, the voices; the likes and the comments; the scrolling and the swiping; the ads and the marketing all seem to be contributing in both tacit and obvious ways to our increasing polarization and isolation from each other. None of it seems to be going away anytime soon.

As Sister Nancy describes it, research confirms that addiction to social media is both physical and psychological, and the negative effect on mental health and low self-esteem are also observable, and crucially so for young people and children.

So what can we do? What must we do to reclaim our health, our attention, our time, and ultimately our souls? How do we detach the digital umbilical cord and make more room to connect with the Divine Healer and our Eternal Redeemer, Jesus Christ?

How can we carve a path to peace within ourselves in order to attain what Saint Paul refers to as the "peace of God, which surpasses all understanding" (Phil 4:7)?

That's where this compelling volume comes in. Sister Nancy has prayerfully and skillfully assembled a powerful, practical, six-week media fasting plan that anyone and everyone can follow. This book will help us take back that time and space we have given up to our brain's reward centers and replace it with the eternal spiritual reward of time spent in the presence and contemplation of the Lord; time spent in the company of others, which strengthens our community and allows us to see each other as whole persons and not just the "best of" we disclose as our digital selves; and time spent cultivating inner peace by centering ourselves in God, our Father and Creator, his Son, Jesus, and his Holy Spirit.

This reclaimed period of recharging will lead us to hope more in he who is our true hope and our true peace.

The variety of options Sister proposes are as diverse as they are personalized. Whether you want to go cold turkey for twenty-four hours or hard-core for a solid month, there's something here for everyone to begin unplugging. Scripture passages followed by daily reflections combine the profound with the relatable. The Prayers of Reparation, the Check-ins, and the Life Hacks are all sharp tools to keep you faithful and focused on your journey to ultimate spiritual health.

As I continue to surrender my own life and career to a deeper relationship with Christ, the demands of that career have inevitably led me to become more reliant on building social media platforms that reach many in order to glorify his message. I have not been exempted from the "swipe and scroll" epidemic that consumes more of my time than I both realize and like to admit. Sister Nancy's work in this book has shown me how even someone whose profession is directly impacted by an active online presence can benefit eternally by implementing a more Christ-centric plan for using social media, and by spending more time in prayer with him in order to truly and completely recharge.

In essence, by being less concerned about how many social media followers I have, with the guidance of this fast, I am more equipped to be a better follower of him whom I serve.

May the Lord bless you, recharge you, and bring you closer to him as you endeavor on your media fast.

—Jonathan Roumie

# Introduction

Do you ever feel sluggish, overwhelmed, or anxious after spending too much time in front of a screen? Do you sometimes feel guilty for spending too much money on your favorite game app? Does your media use negatively affect your relationships with God and others? Is it hard to set aside time for prayer each day? If you answered *yes* to any of these questions, then you're in the right place.

Technology is everywhere. The world runs on it. Life. Work. Entertainment. Relationships. We need our devices to connect. Yet, their constant presence and our continuous attachment to them can be all-consuming. We may also feel uncertain about how our relationship with God is relevant to our media use and how faith can play a role in our media choices. If you have ever experienced these struggles or asked these questions about your media, then a conscious, prayerful break might be helpful. Sometimes we need to detox our brains . . . and our souls!

Living our lives before a screen often leads to a disconnect from ourselves, diminishing our ability to cope and connect meaningfully with others. The fast-paced exchanges and excessive multitasking can leave us feeling fragmented, limiting our attention span on any one task and splitting the way we behave online from the way we act in person. We can also become disconnected from God, who promises true and lasting happiness.

The feeling of disconnect may be a clue that we need to regain a sense of ourselves as human beings, body and soul, and to rediscover the beauty of our relationships. Paying attention to our relationship with God and allowing it to transform how we use our media is essential for our mental and spiritual health if we want to live happy and holy lives. Giving ourselves the space to consider what we most desire and what fulfills our souls can make a difference in how well we live with our technology.

One way to refocus is through media fasting.

# How to Use This Book

THE FIRST PART OF this book explains what fasting is, how to do a media fast, and the many benefits of fasting for the mind, body, and spirit. A guide to create your own fasting plan will help you assess your media experience and determine a plan that works for you.

The second part leads you through six weeks of short daily reflections. These reflections guide you to reflect on your media use, enhance your spiritual life, and support you in your fasting plan. Each week follows a theme: *Paring Down to the Essentials, Choosing the Good Life, Being Media Mindful, Becoming Cultural Mystics, Creating Communion,* and *Transforming the Culture.* The weekly topics build on each other to help you grow in your relationship with Christ and to reconsider your media use through the lens of that relationship. A weekly check-in invites you to test your progress and discern what you learned about yourself and Jesus in the process.

At the end of the book, the *Moving Forward with My Media* section will help you to take the insights and growth of your media fast into your everyday life, so that even when the fast is over, you can find greater peace by centering your media usage more on Christ. The various media prayers and practices in the appendices can help during the fast and long afterward.

Media fasting is an energy boost in your journey toward a healthy and holy existence within the media culture. This book is a guide to recharge your life in Christ and challenge you to live more meaningfully. Remember, changing your media habits takes responsibility, commitment, and sacrifice. Only you can do that for yourself. But all is possible in and through Christ!

# PART 1

# SPIRITUALLY DRAINED

# Blessing and Curse

There are those who let themselves be dragged by the current, but there are always those who direct everything to their own sanctification with joy and with edification.[1]

—*Blessed James Alberione*

MOSES AND THE ISRAELITES had to make a big decision. After escaping Pharaoh and his armies in the land of Egypt, they wandered in the desert for forty years. During that time, the people wearied of following the Lord's commands and worshiped idols. Death and destruction came upon them. God, speaking through Moses, renewed the covenant with his people by offering them two options: "I have set before you life and death, blessings and curses. Choose life so that you and your descendants may live" (Deut 30:19). The blessings of prosperity and life involved loving the Lord and following his commands, knowing that he cares for his people. But if they instead refused to recognize God as Lord of their lives and turned to false gods and idol worship, they would experience the curse of hardship and exile—a path that would lead to death. The Israelites chose life.

Our digital experience can sometimes feel like a blessing or a curse. Media can provide instant access to news and entertainment, connect us with people all over the world, and heighten our awareness of global social issues. They can also cause harm through misuse and overuse. Engaging with false information, gossip, or pornography; believing that self-worth comes from likes and shares; experiencing digital burnout, stress, social isolation, spiritual depletion, and addiction—all these are "curses" we experience when we misuse or overuse our media.

Using media for my ministry and teaching about media, I recognize the blessings of these technologies as amazing gifts of God. But I sometimes feel the curse of too much screen time and its effects on my health, energy, and spiritual well-being. At one point, I realized that my digital devices were distracting me from focusing on what matters to me the most: God! Even my prayer time became riddled with notifications. Constantly distracted, I sensed the Holy Spirit nudging me to give God my whole mind and heart, not allowing my devices to compete for my attention. God invited me to pause and examine my actions. I decided then to fast from my media by setting parameters for daytime use and evening entertainment.

For some people, technology use tends to be moderate and non-problematic. For others, it borders on compulsive and excessive behavior that can become an addiction. The attention-grabbing nature of technologies plus our own weakness can cause us to struggle as we seek to change. Any process of change takes time, commitment, prayer, and patience with ourselves. We change when we recognize the blessing and the curse of our technology and take steps to retrieve the joy of life that God desires for us.

We can choose the blessing by living well with our screens. This involves ensuring that the time we spend using media is well balanced in a way that enhances our relationships with God and others. Otherwise, we may choose the curse by allowing media time to adversely affect our mental and spiritual wellbeing and our relationships, especially our relationship with God. Does our screen use give us life or lead to a disconnected, distracted death of the soul? If we lean toward the latter, it's time to make a change. That is why a media fast can be so helpful.

# What Is Fasting?

What is important is that the strings of our hearts be tuned for the melody which we want to play, that is, the chant, "Glory to God and peace to humanity."[2]

—*Blessed James Alberione*

When we hear the word "fasting," we may think of the common example of dietary fasting. A dietary fast abstains from all or some food or drink at specific periods of time. It can take the form of having two meals a day without snacking, eating smaller portions at meals, or staying away from specific ingredients such as gluten and processed sugar. Wellness websites promote intermittent fasting as a trendy regimen to make healthy choices. A noble practice, fasting strengthens self-control and moderation and can help us live healthier lives. Yet fasting is more than a dietary fad.

Fasting, in the Scriptures, is an act of opening or tuning our heart to God. When facing some significant disaster, the Chosen People fasted to call on God's mercy. Jesus fasted for forty days before starting his public ministry (see Mt 4:2). In the Sermon on the Mount, Jesus says that fasting is an intimate action between us and God.

To open our hearts to God, we can fast from all sorts of things besides food. Fasting as a spiritual discipline involves doing without something that gives us pleasure or in which we over-indulge. This includes our technology. When we fast, we remove distractions, discipline our impulses, and examine our desires and motivations.

Fasting reminds us that only Jesus can fulfill all our deepest longings. He desires an intimate relationship with us. He wants to draw us into his self-communicative love, a love that generates life and holiness. Fasting leads us to a loving relationship with Jesus Christ because it attunes us to his presence in our souls. This is the key. We don't fast for fasting's sake. We fast to better love Jesus and our neighbor—the two greatest commandments. Fasting moves us out of our ego-centric world toward other people. That may all sound idyllic, but fasting requires a commitment that involves some type of sacrifice. It directs us to change our habits through self-discipline and to order our desires to a life of virtue. It's about choosing the good so that we can become the best version of ourselves, the person God created us to be.

A media fast can be challenging, but it's so worth it! By fasting from the media, we learn to do without it, as well as how to live with media in a healthy, balanced way. Fasting is not simply about giving something up and feeling its lack; it is, more importantly, about replacing what we give up with something that gives us life. Remember, God wants all of our minds and hearts! During this fast, we can replace the time we would normally spend on our screens with practices that nurture our relationship with Christ and others, such as prayer, meditation, spiritual reading, or works of mercy (see Appendix D for Spiritual and Corporal Works of Mercy). By setting aside time for an intentional fast, we can grow in understanding the role of digital media in our lives and invite Christ into our experience so to live well with our media moving forward.

# Effects of Media Fasts

Let us not grow tired of fighting against concupiscence.... One of these is addiction to the digital media, which impoverishes human relationships . . . cultivate instead a more integral form of human communication made up of "authentic encounters," face-to-face and in person.[3]

—*Pope Francis*

USUALLY, WHEN WE CHOOSE to embark on an adventure, we do so to seek a benefit for ourselves. Doing a media fast provides many benefits to our physical, mental, and spiritual health.

1. **Connecting with God**—We fast so we can recognize with greater clarity God's grace at work in and around us. Fasting frees us to respond more generously to God, who pours his superabundant love upon us, and to grow in our ability to hear his voice. Eliminating some of the digital clutter from our lives makes room for us to spend time nurturing our relationship with the one who loves us. A strengthened relationship with Christ spills over into our daily life choices, including our media use, helping us make better media choices from this point forward.

2. **Increased energy**—Prolonged screen time can sap energy, especially if it is at night right before going to bed. The light of the screen sends dopamine to the brain, stimulating thought processes that prevent restful sleep. Disrupted sleep resulting from screen

time decreases our energy. Fasting from digital media one hour before bedtime can help us sleep better. We may also choose to limit screen time to take time for physical exercise. Physical activities increase the heart rate, supply oxygen to the blood cells, and so improve energy.

3. **More focus**—Scattered brain functions due to excessive screen use lessen awareness of the task at hand. Notifications and ads distract us and interrupt our focus. The instant gratification and incessant pace of online information decrease our attention spans. Breaking the habit of viewing things online that absorb or scatter our attention can retrain our brains to stay on task and pay attention for longer periods of time. So many drugs on the market offer intensified mental stimulus, but a digital fast is a cheaper and safer way to stimulate the brain and increase focus.

4. **Inner peace**—We sometimes use digital media as a replacement for boredom or an escape from difficult external situations. But filling our minds with disturbing news, violence, online arguments, other people's opinions of us, or content that makes us compare our lives with others' only disturbs our peace. Peace can be restored when we center ourselves in God. Putting aside the phone or other digital devices allows us to notice who and what is around us. We can thank God, the Creator of all, for the beauty we often miss when we're focused on our screens.

5. **Better relationships**—Digital fasts improve our relationships by helping us recognize other people as whole persons, not just the aspects of themselves they present online. We get to know people better the more we spend quality time with them. Paying attention only to our screens prevents us from truly seeing and hearing the other in front of us. Listening is an art. It's a learned practice to hear with our ears what another is saying. To listen with our mind and heart shows interest, concern, care, and love. The more we remove digital distractions while with others, the stronger will be the relationships that add to our quality of life.

# Ways of Media Fasting

Read the book of your own conscience, taking a little time out from useless reading and entertainment.[4]

—*Blessed James Alberione*

How DOES A MEDIA fast work? Just like fasting from food and drink, there are various ways to fast from media. These fasts can be intermittent, especially if we use screens for work or study. A fast can target specific media or apps, or center on conscious choices about what we post online and how often we create and engage with content. A digital detox, which removes the device or app for a significant period, is the most radical fast.

Here are some suggestions:

## Daily Fasts

- Set your phone on "do not disturb" from an hour before going to bed until an hour after you get up in the morning. A substantial amount of time without digital interruptions makes it more possible to have a peaceful evening and a complete night's rest.

- Use a screen time app that will lock you out of your social media or gaming apps at certain times, such as while you are at work or school or before you go to bed.

- Set your phone alarm or a timer for one hour or less to limit your video gaming, YouTube viewing, online reading of web comics or fan fiction sites, or any other online activity.
- Put a cap on in-game purchases for video games. Share your plan with gaming friends so they can help hold you accountable.
- Turn off all music, radio, or podcasts on your daily commute or while exercising.
- Give yourself only certain times during the day when you will check your phone notifications, such as at 9 am, 12 noon, and 6 pm. Silence your notifications so they will not go off at all hours of the day. This way you will avoid interruptions and not feel obliged to check your phone continually.
- Watch only one episode of a streaming series instead of binging the entire season. Plan ahead how many episodes you will watch and stick to it or set a time limit for your daily TV usage.
- Check or post on social media once a day, or only at times when you don't have other obligations. Limit how often you check for new likes or comments.
- When catching up with friends (coffee, lunch, dinner), suggest no phones during your gathering. In a non-aggressive way, challenge the others to go for one hour without checking their phones. See where the conversation goes!

## 24-Hour Fasts

- Turn off all your digital devices and store them away for a complete 24-hour period. Notice how many times you had the urge to turn your phone on during that time.

# Week-Long Fasts

- Stay off all social media for a week. Remove the apps from your phone.
- Avoid playing your favorite video game for one week.
- Turn off the radio when in your car, or fast from listening to music while exercising or doing chores for a week.
- Read a paper book rather than e-books, web comics, or fan-fiction sites.
- Avoid shopping online for a week. Go to a brick and mortar store if you need something.

# Weekend Fasts

- Do a 48-hour complete digital fast. Spend the weekend catching up with friends or family. Don't lock your phone away completely in case you might want to arrange a meeting with friends, but turn off your notifications and disable all apps except the phone and text messaging.
- Fast from all entertainment media for the weekend. Plan an outdoor activity or hands-on project instead.
- Use the time you would normally spend on media for a prayerful activity, such as reading Scripture or going to Eucharistic Adoration.

# Monthly Fasts

- Go for a month without your social media apps on your phone. Only check them when you are on your computer or tablet.
- Avoid that game app that sucks your time by removing it for one month. Evaluate what you did instead of that game.
- Give up watching YouTube videos and do something active instead.
- Shop in local, independent stores rather than online.

## Seasonal Fasts

○ The Church's liturgical season of Lent is six weeks long and Advent is four weeks. Media fasts can be a form of penance during these seasons. Delete problematic apps from your phone. Fast from them for the entire season of Lent or Advent. Use the time you'd spend on screens to add or deepen a spiritual practice (ideas are in the daily meditations).

○ During Lent or Advent, choose the movies or television you will watch and schedule when you will view them. Plan a movie night or watch a streaming show with friends and talk about it afterward using the *Cinema Divina* method (see Appendix D). Keep the other evenings free to meet with friends, attend a Church event, or read a spiritual book.

The type of plan you choose depends on your goals and how you want to invite Christ into your media experience.

# Making a Media Fast Plan

*Any small exploration made with the idea of discovering ourselves brings us closer to the pinnacle of knowledge.*[5]

—*Blessed James Alberione*

To BEGIN, YOU WANT to understand your media habits and identify the goal of your fast. For example, maybe you want to break the habit of impulsively reaching for your phone when you feel bored or unhappy. Or you may wish to have balance in your media use so you can spend more time on your relationships with God and others. Identifying some concrete elements of a digital fast in view of your chosen focus will make the fast more realistic and help you keep to what you've committed.

## Understand your habits

1. Do a media audit. Write down what you did yesterday hour by hour. Notice how much of your day was spent using some form of media versus time spent with other people or doing things unrelated to tech use.

2. Identify the apps and devices that are problematic for you. Write them here and write why they cause problems. (Addictive? Troubling content? Etc.)

3. What are the triggers to your excessive media use? For example, maybe you turn to media when you are feeling bored, lonely, or anxious. Or you have some media always on while doing other things and so are never "off." Other triggers may be hearing your notification bell, seeing ads for new mobile games, allowing the autoplay function on streaming services, or hearing people talk about certain social media accounts or viral posts. List your triggers.

4. Check the screen time function on your phone, computer, or tablet to see how much time you spend on certain apps/devices per day or week.

## State your goal

*What do you want to achieve and why?*

1. Ideally, how much time would you want to spend on specific apps/devices per day? Per week?

2. Is there anything that you want to stop doing completely?

3. Consider what benefits you hope will come from this change (see Effects of Media Fasts, page 11).

# Determine the period of the fast

- o Daily fast
- o 24-hour fast
- o 48-hour fast
- o Weekly fast
- o Monthly fast
- o Seasonal fast (Lent or Advent)

## What it looks like

What will you do to limit access to that problem app/
device?

## Consider alternatives

Consider and list alternatives to time spent on your app/device, such as establishing regular prayer time, picking up a new or old hobby, exercising and/or spending time outdoors, or reading a paper-based book.

## Concrete actions

Make a list of concrete actions that will help you achieve your purpose. For example, you could invite a friend to do the fast with you or ask someone to hold you accountable during your fast.

## Predict obstacles

Predict obstacles that may arise and ways you will overcome those obstacles. For example, if you know you might drop this fast on the first weekend, plan your weekend activities ahead, or if you think you may turn to your device out of habit, put a note on your device to remind you of your fast.

| Obstacles that may arise: | Ways I will respond to each obstacle: |
|---|---|
| | |
| | |
| | |
| | |
| | |

# Sample Plan

### Understand your habits

1. Do a media audit. Write down what you did yesterday hour by hour. Notice how much of your day was spent using some form of media versus time spent with other people or doing things unrelated to tech use.

I spent the first two hours of the morning getting ready for the day, during which I checked my phone briefly for messages, the day's weather forecast, and the traffic report. On the way to work, I listened to a podcast for about half an hour. During the morning at work, I checked my phone a few times when I got email notifications. Most of these were brief, but one of these times I spent about 15 minutes deleting junk emails and scrolling through "recommended for you" articles. During my lunch break, I checked Instagram and Facebook and then read the daily news on my phone. I found an interesting article, so I continued reading articles on the news site for half an hour after my lunch break ended. Mid-afternoon, I finished a task and checked my phone for a "mental break," which turned into spending 20 minutes on Reddit. On the way home from work, I called my mom and we talked for about half an hour; then I listened to the radio for the rest of the drive. After dinner, I watched an hour of TV with my family, but I was only partially paying attention to the show and to my family because I checked social media again during the commercial breaks. Afterward, I wrote in my prayer journal for about 20 minutes. I planned to go to bed after that, but when I turned my phone on to put it on silent for the night, I noticed a friend had sent me a link to a YouTube video, so I watched several more videos for about 45 more minutes until I went to bed.

2. Identify the apps and devices that are problematic for you. Write them here and write why they cause problems. (Addictive? Troubling content? Etc.).

> I have the most trouble with my phone. I sometimes use my phone to look up something specific but then end up scrolling compulsively. I also sometimes check social media on my phone during times that cut into my work hours or family time. I often find that even if I am looking at my phone or social media for a specific purpose, it can trigger excessive scrolling if I don't consciously stop myself, and I can have trouble getting back on task.

3. What are the triggers to your excessive media use? For example, maybe you turn to media when you are feeling bored, lonely, or anxious. Or you have some media always on while doing other things and so are never "off." Other triggers may be hearing your notification bell, seeing ads for new mobile games, allowing the autoplay function on streaming services, or hearing people talk about certain social media accounts or viral posts. List your triggers.

> I check my phone and social media accounts when I need a "mental break," such as when I am transitioning between tasks at work or when I get home in the evening and want to relax. Sometimes I do so when I am trying to avoid something I don't want to deal with, such as an unpleasant task at work or a difficult emotion or situation. When I hear about an interesting news story or social media post, sometimes I drop whatever else I'm doing and check for it right away, then get sucked in by related or "recommended for you" content.

4. Check the screen time function on your phone, computer, or tablet to see how much time you spend on certain apps/devices per day or week.

> Over the past week, I spent an average of three hours on my phone per day. I spent the most time on Instagram (45 minutes per day), news sites (40 minutes per day), and YouTube (30 minutes per day).

## State your goal

*What do you want to achieve and why?*

1. Ideally, how much time would you want to spend on specific apps/devices per day? Per week?

> Ideally, I would like to use my phone for about one hour per day (outside of making necessary phone calls, using GPS, etc.). I would like to spend no more than 20 minutes per day on each individual social media app or website.

2. Is there anything that you want to stop doing completely?

> I want to stop checking or scrolling on my phone/social media while I am with other people, especially when I am spending time with my family in the evenings and on weekends.

3. Consider what benefits you hope will come from this change (see Effects of Media Fasts, page 11).

> I want to use my phone more intentionally (not just scrolling for the sake of scrolling). I want to be aware of

why I compulsively reach for my phone or continue to use it after I have already finished whatever I needed to do, so that I can better understand how to combat those temptations. I also want to set clearer boundaries around when I check my phone or social media and how much time I spend doing this, so that I can be more present to the people around me and more focused at work.

## Determine the period of the fast

○ Daily fast
○ 24-hour fast
○ 48-hour fast
○ Weekly fast
○ Monthly fast
○ Seasonal fast (Lent or Advent)

I will do a daily fast for a six-week period.

## What it looks like

What will you do to limit access to that problem app/device?

I will fast completely from social media for the full six weeks. I will only check news stories and personal (non-work-related) email during my lunch break at work and after dinner, chores, and family time in the evenings. On weekends, I will also check these apps/sites only once a day when I do not have other obligations. During times of work, prayer, or socializing with others, I will put my phone on silent and keep it out of reach. During times when I can use my phone, I will put it on vibrate so that I can hear when I get a message and will not be tempted to check it compulsively to see whether I've missed any notifications.

## Consider alternatives

Consider and list alternatives to time spent on your app/device, such as establishing regular prayer time, picking up a new or old hobby, exercising and/or spending time outdoors, or reading a paper-based book.

To make sure I don't keep scrolling excessively after my lunch break at work, I will take a short walk every day after lunch. Instead of checking my phone as a "mental break" between tasks, I will pause and say a short prayer. During my free time on the weekends, I will take some of the time I would otherwise spend reading social media content or news stories and spend it reading a physical book.

## Concrete actions

Make a list of concrete actions that will help you achieve your purpose. For example, you could invite a friend to do the fast with you or ask someone to hold you accountable during your fast.

I will write out my fasting plan and put it somewhere I can see it daily. I will also share my plan with a friend who is good at accountability and ask her to check on me once a week.

## Predict obstacles

Predict obstacles that may arise and ways you will overcome those obstacles. For example, if you know you might drop this fast on the first weekend, plan your weekend activities ahead, or if you think you may turn to your device out of habit, put a note on your device to remind you of your fast.

| Obstacles that may arise: | Ways I will respond to each obstacle: |
|---|---|
| I will compulsively reach for my phone to check for notifications during times my phone is within reach. | I will put a sticky note on my phone to remind myself to stop and pray, or to ask myself why I am reaching for my phone. |

| *Obstacles that may arise:* | *Ways I will respond to each obstacle:* |
|---|---|
| The change in routine and the extra free time on weekends will make it harder to limit how much time I spend on my phone. | I will plan in-person social activities on some weekends. On other weekends or when I need quiet time to relax, I will either take a walk outside or make sure I have a new or exciting book to read. |
| I may be tempted to make exceptions to my fasting plan if I hear about an important news story or social media post. | I will "bookmark" the story to look at it at a time when I do not have other obligations. To be mindful of the amount of time I spend checking for new comments or related content, I will pause to reflect and pray about the story or post before I read or watch any new content about it. |

# Getting Started

ONCE YOU'VE CREATED A plan, you're ready to begin the six-week challenge to reflect on your media experience. The daily reflections can assist you in discerning the way you currently interact with your technology and what long-term changes you want to make. You will also look at those deep yearnings that tug at your heart in moments of silence and reflection. Each day's reflection ends with a prayer, asking God for his mercy and grace.

At the end of each week, you will do a check-in on your fasting plan to evaluate your progress and assess those areas that still need your attention. There are also weekly prayers of reparation for the ways in which the media are misused. Reparation is making amends for sins (either our own or others') that insult God and his goodness. Praying in reparation for the ways in which the media are misused makes amends for those who create or use the media in ways that dehumanize or lead others to sin. The weekly check-ins also include inspirational thoughts and practical tips to provide encouragement and support needed to keep you going during the fast.

So, are you ready for the challenge? Let's do this!

# PART 2

# SPIRITUAL RECHARGE

# WEEK 1

# Paring Down to the Essentials

"Blow the trumpet [. . .] sanctify a fast" (Joel 2:15), says the prophet. . . . It is a summons to stop—a "halt!"—, to focus on what is essential, to fast from the unnecessary things that distract us. It is a wake-up call for the soul.[6]

—*Pope Francis*

REMOVING *STUFF* FROM OUR lives has become a cultural trend. People push against the throwaway culture of consumerism by moving into tiny houses, living off the grid, and buying from thrift stores. Some people even remove digital technologies from their lives. This is because we recognize that the *stuff* of our lives often clutters our homes and our hearts. We sometimes find the need to pare down to the essentials to return to the familiar and the simple.

The changes we make to unclutter our lives are based on our core beliefs and values. Our values ground us so that we can live authentically. Authenticity means being the best version of ourselves, that is, a person who lives by values that guide virtuous behavior. These values determine what matters the most to us in life—for example, family, friendship, compassion, honesty, kindness, and truth. The Gospel values Jesus teaches us through his words and example push us even farther to live as *exceptional* human beings. He asks us not only to love our neighbor, but to love our enemy. He asks us to continually forgive those who have insulted us. To be kind is to be a good human being, but to give of ourselves in sacrificial love after Jesus' example is to be *exceptional*. And holiness is exceptional. Gospel values help us to become not only good persons, but saints!

## The "Stuff" of Our Lives

Examining our core values can help us determine whether we really value our relationship with God more highly than anything else. When we know what we value, we can consider what *stuff* prevents us from living according to our values and finding fulfillment in God alone. The *stuff* of our lives may be not only material things, but also attitudes and ways of behavior that don't lead to union with God.

As human beings with a body and a soul, we live in the natural world while our hearts yearn for what is supernatural—for something more than this world can offer us. This yearning tugs at our consciousness, especially when we try to satisfy it by cluttering our lives with the pursuit of likes, followers, or gaming scores. Those may satisfy us outwardly, but our souls yearn for a peace not found solely in the things of this world.

The desire for God will often lead us to pare down, since when we encounter the Divine we see the futility of the material *stuff* we acquire. We begin to realize why the *stuff* of this world cannot completely satisfy this desire. "You have made us for yourself, O Lord, and our heart is restless until it rests in you," as Saint Augustine observes. We long for "something more" that stretches us to reach for the spiritual. We yearn for God. Nurturing this relationship with God motivates us to unclutter our hearts to make room for him.

# Transformation in Christ

As we pare down our media experiences, we may begin to recognize a need for the grace of transformation in Christ—that is, a need for change that leads us to become more like Christ through the way we live each day. We are the most Christ-like when we become the best version of ourselves. In emptying our lives of some of the clutter, we gain room to receive what's most important and what leads to fulfillment. This challenge is hard; it needs the discipline of seeking authenticity.

To be authentically human is to be Christ-like, since Jesus, who is the Way, shows us what true humanity looks like. Through his own self-giving love, he reveals to us the best of humanity, and he calls us to act as he did. We come to this level of sacrificial love through fasting and focusing on our relationship with him. Fasting helps us to see our selfish behaviors that need the grace of conversion—behaviors that may include our media choices. When we pare down to the essentials of life, we give Jesus space to be the Truth to which our core values point and the Life that will guide us on the path to God.

*WEEK 1  SUNDAY*

# Between Me and God

"When you fast, put oil on your head and wash your face, so that your fasting may be seen not by others but by your Father who is in secret; and your Father who sees in secret will reward you."

*—Matthew 6:17–18*

HAVE YOU EVER BEEN surprised by someone posting something personal on social media? There is a fine line between being authentic and oversharing. We all want love and acceptance. But does that come only from online recognition? As we delve into our fast and consider our relationship with God, we can begin to take stock of the motivations behind our use of media. Oversharing the details of our lives online comes from a desire to be noticed, which can be a form of pride. Excessive preoccupation with what other people think of us leads to a destructive self-centeredness. Jesus tells us that God notices us and accepts us. His attention is what matters.

Jesus also encourages us to keep our spiritual practices, such as fasting, between us and God. When we begin this media fast, we might be tempted to overshare about it on social media as another way to be noticed and seen as "holy." If we do post that we will stay away from social media for a while, we can share with others the reason for our absence: for example, we could say that we are seeking to be our best selves online, which requires intermittent breaks. We may also share about our fast to keep ourselves accountable. But Jesus' words challenge us to examine our hearts to determine whether our fast leads to boasting in order to appear holier than others. Are we more concerned about what others think of us than what God thinks? Paring down to the essentials reminds us to be aware of our motivations. It helps us grow closer to God so his voice and guidance in our souls becomes more prominent, while the *stuff* of life and others' opinions of us become less so. It is more important to focus on our relationship with God than on relationships with people online whom we want to admire us.

Fasting is not an opportunity for proclaiming to the world everything about our lives. It is a time to focus our heart and mind on Christ. After the fast, sharing what we have learned can be helpful for someone else seeking the courage to do the same. But our present journey of fasting is ultimately about our personal relationship with God.

If you haven't made a fasting plan yet, you can take this first week to do so. Begin this week by considering what your fast entails and what you will do in place of time spent on your media. You may want to use that time usually spent on a screen to call a friend or to sit quietly with God in prayer.

*Jesus, I desire to grow closer to you during this fast. Humble my heart so I keep the details of my media fast between us. Give me the grace to be faithful to this sacrifice so my love and reliance on you may increase each day.*

# True Greatness

Athletes exercise self-control in all things; they do it to receive a perishable wreath, but we an imperishable one. So I do not run aimlessly, nor do I box as though beating the air; but I punish my body and enslave it, so that after proclaiming to others I myself should not be disqualified.

—*1 Corinthians 9:25–27*

ATHLETES ARE HIGHLY DISCIPLINED people. To achieve greatness in a sport requires determination and commitment. The film *The Boys in the Boat* tells the true story of the University of Washington's eight-man crew team who defied the world's expectations. The rowers were sons of loggers, farmers, and factory workers struggling to survive during the Great Depression. Through fierce training and sheer determination, they went up against the more experienced and wealthy teams of Harvard, Penn, and Cal State, not only to win the National title but to go on to face the greatest crew teams in the world at the 1936 Berlin Olympics. Under the gaze of Adolf Hitler, the underdog team from the Northwest came from behind to capture the gold medal and their place in history. It is at once a most heartbreaking and thrilling movie about some poor college guys who had nothing to lose and found greatness. That same tenacity and discipline are required in deepening a relationship with God.

As we become aware of our spiritual longings, we may realize that we're yearning for something more than what we've achieved in life so far. We long for something new—for greatness. We are enticed by a desire to fill the emptiness in our souls. Yet we may hesitate to begin. Starting calls for commitment and "self-control in all things," as Saint Paul says.

Asceticism is a spiritual self-discipline that trains the body and the mind to seek the desires of the spirit. Kneeling in prayer, for example, is a form of asceticism that trains our body to take a humble posture before God. Ascetic practices such as praying and fasting are not about punishing ourselves, but rather about learning discipline so we can make good choices and become the best version of ourselves. Our media fasting plan and other practices help us in this process of spiritual self-discipline. Exercising positive behaviors helps us to replace our negative digital habits and turn our hearts and minds to Christ so we can attain the *imperishable crown* Saint Paul speaks about. The more we practice self-discipline during this fast, the easier it will become and the easier it will be to use media virtuously once the fast is over. Through the asceticism of fasting, the greatness we seek becomes possible, since we have made room in our hearts for Christ, who fulfills every longing.

Take a moment now to reflect on what practices of spiritual self-discipline can help you focus on your relationship with Christ, who calls you to greatness.

*Jesus, give me the grace and discipline to change my media habits, leaving behind my old ways so that I achieve the greatness you desire of me.*

# Tuning Out Chaos

"Peace I leave with you; my peace I give to you. I do not give to you as the world gives. Do not let your hearts be troubled, and do not let them be afraid."

—*John 14:27*

STANDING IN LINE AT the grocery store one day, I became aware of all the digital noise around me: music playing over the speakers, videos advertising products, scanners beeping at checkouts, and my phone ringing with multiple notifications. I felt I was in a vacuum of electronic chaos.

Life can overwhelm us when we feel unable to control the incessant digital noise. Sometimes the sense of being out of control comes from too much data crowding our brain. We don't have time or energy to deal with every text, news story, or social media post. To gain some sense of control, our ego may tempt us to think that we need to solve every problem or answer every notification. But in reality, that may make us feel even more out of control.

With all the digital sounds surrounding us, it is easy to lose our sense of inner peace. In this chaos, our hearts long for silence, for space in which to rest and reflect. When the cacophony of digital voices overwhelms us, we can consider this a reminder to "turn down the volume." We do this by fasting from our media, or even when we are not fasting, by setting limits on what we engage with and how much time we give it. Most importantly, we can tune in to the voice that matters—the voice of the Lord—by offering him all that overwhelms us, trusting that he can handle it. When we turn over all our concerns to him, we can rest in peaceful assurance.

Christ's presence in our lives changes things. Jesus emphasizes to his disciples that he is the source of their peace. Unlike the world's sense of peace, which is only a superficial lack of chaos, his peace is deep and abiding. The more we listen to his voice, the more we discover we can be serene even in the midst of the world's turmoil. When we surrender control to Jesus, turning to him in trust, his peace transforms our hearts. The Lord is greater than all our digital demands. He holds the world in his loving embrace.

Take some time today to sit in silence without any digital devices and pray several times, "*Jesus, I surrender myself to you; take care of everything!*"

*Jesus, sometimes so many voices drown out your peace in my heart. Teach me to "turn down" these voices. Give me the grace to always choose to listen to your voice. Help my faith in you to grow so that I may believe that you are more powerful than any situation or challenge I face. Jesus, I trust in you!*

*WEEK 1 WEDNESDAY*

# Instagramification

We do not dare to classify or compare ourselves with some of those who commend themselves. But when they measure themselves by one another, and compare themselves with one another, they do not show good sense.

—*2 Corinthians 10:12*

SAINT PAUL SAW PEOPLE in the Corinthian community comparing themselves with each other to judge who was the better follower of Christ. In today's Scripture, Paul comes right out and tells the Corinthians that people who boast of their accomplishments or compare themselves with others regarding holiness or popularity are not living as true disciples of Jesus.

On social media, this insidious temptation to create comparisons can be manifested in two ways: feeling envious of those who are more popular or appear more successful online, or creating idealized versions of ourselves to receive attention. Even though we know that social media only allows us to see fragments of the lives of others, we can easily be tempted to compare our lives with the versions of others' lives that we see online. Some influencers may reach "fame" status through the instagramified lifestyles their posts portray, while other people we follow use social media to share their big life accomplishments—such as getting married, buying a dream house, or landing the perfect job—leaving us feeling envious. Constantly comparing ourselves with others destroys the sense we should have of our dignity as beloved children of God. Our sense of others' dignity also suffers when we are tempted to see them as threats or competitors.

The temptation to compare can also manifest itself in how we use media to increase attention to ourselves over and above other people. "Instagramification" describes the phenomenon of people posting idealized snippets and altered images from their lives to receive attention. It is hard not to give undue importance to how many people "like" us or "follow" us. However, we can only keep up a "perfect" online persona for so long. Our popularity in life and online will change according to the perceptions of others—perceptions that may or may not reflect reality. Instagramified posts don't reflect what is really happening in our lives or the reality of our dignity and value in the eyes of God.

The next time we feel tempted to feel sorry for ourselves when seeing the fame or success of others, we can remember how fleeting notoriety is and that it is more important to recognize what is truly essential. We can also remember that using media to show only idealized versions of ourselves perpetuates comparisons and doesn't show the truth and beauty of identity as God's child.

Take some quiet moments now to consider these truths: how God sees you is more important than how the world sees you. The God who lovingly created you knows and loves you for who you truly are, and he wants to be close to you. He created you for a reason, giving you a unique mission that no one else can carry out. Pray today for the grace to be authentic online.

*Jesus, Image of the Father, show me my incomparable worth in your eyes that no online presence can change. Let me be content with my true self and believe that you have a definite purpose for my life.*

# Facing Burnout

"Therefore I tell you, do not worry about your life, what you will eat or what you will drink, or about your body, what you will wear. Is not life more than food, and the body more than clothing? Look at the birds of the air; they neither sow nor reap nor gather into barns, and yet your heavenly Father feeds them. Are you not of more value than they? And can any of you by worrying add a single hour to your span of life?"

—*Matthew 6:25–27*

IN THIS WIRED EXISTENCE we may experience the constant pressure to be "on" all the time, both professionally and personally. We may feel the unspoken expectation to be a social influencer with millions of followers seeking relationship advice. Or we might want to be the person with the perfect gaming score everyone envies. Even if we don't feel compelled to be famous, we may still feel pressured to always present an idealized version of ourselves online or to prove that our opinions are the right ones. We may fret about not being talented, sociable, or amusing enough for everyone to pay attention to or admire. Such an attitude can add stress to our lives. If we are an influencer, we may wonder how we can "turn off" for a time to collect ourselves. Even if we are not an influencer, we may wonder how we can pull back from the online pressure to be noticed.

Living our lives online, trying to maintain our image, is an unpredictable business. Human beings are fickle. We may be the popular social influencer at one moment, yet at the very next, our followers have moved on to the next personality. Or one moment we may be the gaming score leader and the next moment we're at the bottom. This lifestyle of maintaining an on-demand digital existence draws on our mental and physical reserves, sometimes leading to burnout. It's time during this media fast to assess our own internal expectations and personal stress.

Anxiety disorders affect almost 20 percent of the adult population in the U.S.[7] and almost 25 percent in Canada.[8] Researchers have seen a significant increase in mental health conditions among young adults, coinciding with the increasing popularity of social media.[9] In cases of chronic or debilitating anxiety disorders that disrupt our daily lives, medical attention is needed. But whether our stress is the result of an anxiety disorder, digital burnout, or a combination of factors, it's important to deal with it and to pay attention to our souls. There are many effective natural and spiritual means for dealing with stress. These are my top five: sufficient sleep; exercise and nutritious diet; regulated media use; prayer and meditation; and reception of the sacraments. The grace we receive by participating in the Eucharistic Liturgy, reading the word of God, going to Confession, and reciting the Rosary and other prayers is unrivaled for the spiritual healing of mind and body.

Jesus says repeatedly, "Do not be afraid" and "do not worry about your life." Our worry stems from our desire to control life and everything around us when we really have no control. Only God is in control. This attitude is reflected in the phrase popularized by Alcoholics Anonymous: *let go and let God.* This is true for everyone. One aspect of letting go that we can apply to our media fast is to "let go" of our devices or some form of media that may cause us anxiety. Letting go of our worries about life, as Jesus says in the Gospel of Matthew, means that we can trust our Heavenly Father to support us and provide for our needs.

––––––––––○○○––––––––––

One of the best prayers in time of anxiety is: *Jesus, I trust in you!* Take some time today to pray this simple prayer repeatedly. In the future you might pray it whenever you feel overwhelmed by the pressures of life.

*God our Father, I'm burned out. The pressures of living my life online have left me feeling anxious and mentally exhausted. I desire to surrender my life to you. Help me believe that I am worth everything to you.*

*WEEK 1 FRIDAY*

# iGods

> See to it that no one takes you captive through philoso-
> phy and empty deceit, according to human tradition, ac-
> cording to the elemental spirits of the universe, and not
> according to Christ.
>
> *—Colossians 2:8*

IN THE EARLY CHURCH, the Colossians were caught up with the philosophical ideologies and idols of their day, many of which were directly opposed to Christian beliefs about God, the human person, and creation. Today many ideologies and idols of our media culture conflict with our beliefs in the One God.

TV shows like *The Voice* and other talent competitions portray those contestants with special talents and abilities as pop culture *idols*. What is the real meaning of *idols*? An *idol* is defined as an object of intense devotion. To whom or what do we give our extreme devotion?

God makes it clear to Moses in the Book of Exodus that his people are to worship the Lord alone. God says, "I am the Lord your God, who brought you out of the land of Egypt, out of the house of slavery; you shall have no other gods before me" (Ex 20:2–3). We may say to ourselves that we have no idols. Yet, idols present themselves to us in many ways. An *idol* may be a celebrity, an academic degree, a career goal, money, popularity, or the number of social followers we have.

God made us and loved us into being. He alone deserves our worship. When we admire the talent of another, it is God that we adore. Each of us has been created out of love to be love and to give our love to God in return. Each person is God's unique creation. We can esteem gifted people, but only God deserves our worship and praise.

Your media fast helps you reassess whom or what you admire and why. This is part of paring down to the essentials. Today, consider the time and attention you give to whatever you may be fixating on that takes the place of God in your life. Then reflect on how much time you give to worship of God. Today may be the opportunity to reevaluate your priorities in order to become a more authentic human being created by Love Itself.

*Lord, our God, you are all great and all holy. You alone do I praise, worship, and adore. Help me to focus my life and desires only on you, who can satisfy all my desires for recognition and love.*

*WEEK 1 SATURDAY*

# Digital Detox

Do not worry about anything, but in everything by prayer and supplication with thanksgiving let your requests be made known to God. And the peace of God, which surpasses all understanding, will guard your hearts and your minds in Christ Jesus.

*—Philippians 4:6–7*

I RECENTLY DISCOVERED THE Global Day of Unplugging.[10] Yep, there's a day for that! It was started by a Jewish group to challenge people to digitally unplug for a 24-hour period on the first Friday of March. Now it's a worldwide event.

Our brains are amazing organs. We consciously manage only sixty bits of information per second, but our brains also process more than eleven million bits per second of messages from our body. Physically, this is normal for us, but emotionally and mentally we're limited. That's why it's helpful to periodically reconsider our online engagement, especially during this media fast. The sheer amount of information online and sometimes the excessive toxic verbiage on social media can leave us feeling interiorly and physically drained—in need of a digital detox.

Consciously regaining interior peace may take some effort. For example, we could inhabit smaller and more intimate digital spaces, such as private groups or chat rooms that could foster meaningful relationships through respectful dialogue. To make this happen we might have to become facilitators, but the effort would be rewarding and supportive of our mental and spiritual health. We might be surprised to learn how many other people feel the same way!

Another antidote to digital overload is Christian meditation. Our culture often understands meditation as developing self-awareness to obtain perspective or achieve mental clarity. But such a definition remains self-centered. Christian meditation is a structured prayer to become aware of God's revelations—for example, in the Scriptures. This type of meditation allows us to heighten our awareness of reality in relation to God, our loving Father. We become open to relying on God instead of on ourselves. Saint Paul suggests that meditation and prayer lead to awareness and peace when he says, "Do not worry about anything . . . let your requests be made known to God. And the peace of God . . . will guard your hearts and minds in Christ Jesus." That is so reassuring!

Try meditating on a passage from the Scriptures, such as the Gospel of Luke's storm at sea (8:22–25). As you read and reflect on the passage, picture yourself in the scene, contemplating Christ's words and actions as if they are meant for you.

*Lord and Savior, I want a deeper relationship with you. Purify my mind from digital rubbish and lead me to reflect on your word to me, for I seek the peace that can only come from you.*

# Media Fast Check-in

How's your media fast going? What elements of the fast have been the easiest to keep or the most helpful? Which have been the most difficult? Are there some elements of the fast that you haven't kept? What factors led to those difficulties?

## Prayer in Reparation for the Misuse of the Media

*Jesus, I unite myself to you who offered yourself for our salvation, in reparation for the errors and scandals spread throughout the world through the misuse of the media. Through my fasting sacrifice and prayer, may you transform the digital culture so that the media may always be used to support the good of each person and the common good. May every media creation uplift the sacred dignity of every human person, especially the poor and most vulnerable, bringing light, hope, and solidarity to our world. Amen.*

## You Can Do This

Sometimes we may feel anxious at the beginning of our fast because of the challenge to persevere. Continue with the commitment from this point forward, trusting in God's grace. Discouragement can unsettle us, but God is ready to enlighten our next step on the journey.

> The Lord lights the lamps on the road ahead, as and when they are needed; he does not light them all immediately, in the beginning, when they are not yet needed. He does not waste light; but he gives it always at the opportune time.[11]
>
> —Blessed James Alberione

## Life Hack for the Week

Put your devices on "do not disturb" for sleep and work time, giving you focused rest and productivity.

# WEEK 2

# Choosing the Good Life

We must be aware of the reality of life, the little, simple, small progress made each day towards a meditated, desired, counseled, definite goal. We do not live by dreams but begin at the rank and file level and proceed along the slow, sure road of the virtuous.

*—Blessed James Alberione[12]*

As CHILDREN, WE MAY have been asked what we wanted to be when we grew up. Some of the kids in my third-grade class wanted to be superheroes. Sure, the life of a superhero seemed ideal. But I felt I didn't know enough about the world to make that decision at eight years old. What I did realize was that I wanted to be happy—I wanted what I envisioned as "the good life." Comic book superheroes presented a glimpse of what I was looking for, but I wanted more.

I was taught from an early age that happiness comes from being close to God and acting in a manner that pleases him. I learned the virtues of kindness, respect, obedience, charity, and forgiveness. At times, I did not live up to these virtues, but I knew that if I did choose virtue, I felt at peace and believed God would bless me for choosing the good.

When we're young, we're asked about *what* we want to do with our lives, but not *how* we want to live our lives to attain true happiness. The culture says we find it in fortune, fame, and social influence by following our dreams. We may achieve some of that, but does it lead to genuine, lasting happiness? Authentic happiness, which is more than passing pleasure, comes from living "the good life," that is, a morally upright life in relationship with a loving God. The Greek philosopher Aristotle calls the good life a "well-lived life of balance and reason." He says the secret for attaining happiness is virtue.

## Habits of the Soul

Virtues are acquired habits for the good of our whole selves. Attaining them takes time, practice, and perseverance, like anything that requires discipline—such as sports, music, or acting. Practicing the virtues trains our souls to seek the good. Virtues such as patience, courage, self-control, or gentleness draw people to God because they are attractive and desirable for a "good life." People who live virtuously embody the ideal of holiness that Jesus calls us to when he says, "follow me" (Mt 19:21).

Jesus understands that we have to struggle to choose virtue—that this can sometimes seem to be a superhuman ideal. However, in the Gospels, he shows us that virtue is possible with the help of God's grace. His infinite patience with the apostles when they argue about who is the greatest among them (see Lk 22:24–26) reveals his understanding. He tells them that the greatest is not the one with prestige and power, but the servant of all. And when Peter asks him how often he should forgive someone who offends him, Jesus says *always*, and he gives the example on the cross: "Father, forgive them; for they do not know what they are doing" (Lk 23:34). He speaks with merciful love to the woman caught in adultery when everyone else is ready to throw stones. Jesus lays out the path for us and never tires of presenting opportunities to choose "the good life" that he offers in love.

# Choosing the Good

We are wired to seek a good, fruitful, and meaningful life, but due to our wounded human nature, it takes effort for us to recognize and choose what is truly good. We gain wisdom by observing good examples, choosing trustworthy mentors, and learning from our own experiences of trial and error. Wisely selecting media that benefits us means asking ourselves what kinds of media and messages we want to allow into our souls. It requires skill to recognize and choose the good and to avoid media that have a negative influence on us.

We can recognize the good that God desires us to follow by paying attention to the interior movements of our heart. These movements are deeper than surface emotions. They are the fruits of the Holy Spirit: peace, patience, kindness, love, joy, generosity, faithfulness, gentleness, and self-control. Sometimes choosing virtue over our natural desires can be difficult and may not result in immediate happiness, but in the long run we will discover greater interior peace. The fruits of the Holy Spirit offer a clue that we are following God's will in our daily decisions. Choosing the good that God desires for us is the choice of moral excellence, which is virtue.

Making wise choices also involves discovering what God intends for us. Through discernment, we can understand and judge everyday circumstances and daily choices in view of our greater spiritual good, to think as God does and see our lives in relation to God's plan for us. Sometimes we may have to choose between two apparent goods. Discernment practices help us to make choices for the greater good of ourselves and others.

# Digital Virtues

Developing wisdom in daily circumstances allows us to engage with our media in a thoughtful manner. We don't have to eliminate our media to practice a life of balance and reason. Carrying our pursuit of virtue into our media experience also makes the Gospel ideal a reality.

Certain virtues are especially helpful to cultivate and apply in dealing with our media. Temperance is the exercise of self-control to obtain a balanced and disciplined use of all good things. Digital media are created to keep our attention, so it takes self-control to limit our use to what is necessary or possible while accomplishing our other duties. Prudence is the ability to be cautious before acting—for example, to reflect on how we might respond to an emotion-laden text and what the consequences of our response could be. Justice is fairness in recognizing that there are always two sides to a story, which can help us see that we may not have the whole picture when reading internet news or considering social media disputes. Fortitude is courage in the face of adversity, such as speaking the truth when it's unpopular or calling out cyberbullies in video games or other online forums.

We live the Gospel ideal when we exemplify virtue in pursuit of "the good life." That life is what Jesus desires for us. During our media fast, the extra time we take for prayer and reflection will help us grow in virtuous living so we can apply these virtues in our online experience.

WEEK 2 SUNDAY

# Personal Integrity

Timothy, guard what has been entrusted to you. Avoid the profane chatter and contradictions of what is falsely called knowledge; by professing it some have missed the mark as regards the faith.

—1 Timothy 6:20–21

SOMETIMES SOCIAL MEDIA POSTS exhibit the most outrageous virtue signaling. People who record themselves giving a homeless person a sandwich while paying to boost their views draw ire from fellow social media users. The comments attacking the poster are often as offensive as the post is disingenuous. The abuse of a human being's plight for another person's fame is downright appalling and offends against human dignity, as do snarky, uncharitable comments. This type of content online is more about attention-seeking than about virtue. But it can lead us to question how we show virtue and integrity online.

The potential to entertain, unite, and distract all at the same time makes social media intriguing, but it can also affect our ability to grow in virtue. The content we consume may sometimes leave us feeling empty, unsettled, or discouraged. What we allow into our heads can negatively affect our thoughts in ways that hinder growth in virtue. We may need to consider what we allow into our minds and souls. How much of the digital chatter supports our living a virtuous life?

Paul tells Timothy to guard his mind and heart against the superficial and profane talk of popular culture. So much online gossip focuses on superficial materialism or other people's personal relationships. Our faith calls us to draw upon our Christian values and virtues to determine what media to engage with and how. We are to seek the truth that saves, and that means avoiding "what is falsely called knowledge." Reflecting on what content helps us live virtuously may mean discerning whether the accounts we follow inspire and support our pursuit of "the good life." It may also mean exercising personal integrity online by deciding what we choose to engage with when no one is looking.

Today, consider what digital chatter consumes you and how it affects you. Let the content you engage with be such that builds up, promotes joy, and expresses the goodness of a virtuous life.

*Lord, my Savior, free me from the endless chatter of social media that leaves me feeling empty. Show me how or where I can grow in personal integrity online and help me to engage virtuously with online content. Guide me to use my online presence to build up others, bring humor to anxious hearts, and offer hope to a world that longs for fulfillment.*

*WEEK 2 MONDAY*

# Sharing Good News

Finally, beloved, whatever is true, whatever is honorable, whatever is just, whatever is pure, whatever is pleasing, whatever is commendable, if there is any excellence and if there is anything worthy of praise, think about these things.

*—Philippians 4:8*

SAINT PAUL'S LETTER TO the Philippians encourages them to live noble lives by making good moral choices. He lays out the Christian's life of virtue when he says to think about the pure, honorable, just, and holy matters of life. Choosing the good is about what is good not only for ourselves, but also for the entire community. Doing this, Paul implies, leads to the "good life."

The internet presents us with an instantaneous snapshot of what is going on in the world—the good and the evil. Saint Paul's words above are inspiring, but sometimes we find them hard to put into practice when the "bad news" seems to outweigh the "good news" we encounter, or when there are more bad than good things going on in our own lives. But that's when a virtuous Christian response comes in. To share good news online while acknowledging the suffering and pain of humanity is to support a balanced view of reality and call forth a Christian response to human struggle. The noble actions of selfless people working in challenging situations provide a glimpse into the goodness within human beings. We thrive on stories about people who show kindness or do heroic deeds.

I was inspired by the life of Sister Maria Rosa Leggol, often described as the "Mother Teresa of Honduras." Orphaned at age six, she spent her life for Christ by serving the poor and orphaned children of Honduras, helping more than 87,000 to receive food, shelter, education, and especially the love of Christ. The film *With This Light* shows Sister Maria Rosa's life and the goodness emanating from her. Though inspiring, the film also portrays the injustices and challenges faced by the poor and calls us to act courageously like Sister Maria Rosa by doing something for the people in our midst. By sharing this story online, we communicate the truth that God's light shines even in the dark corners of our human experience.

Living a life of virtue online does not mean focusing exclusively on the positive, but engaging with everything authentically human in a Christ-like way. That includes stories of suffering, sin, and pain. As Saint Paul says, we can think about these things with compassion and empathy.

It takes virtue to face the suffering in the world and respond with good, as Sister Maria Rosa has done. Living virtuously helps us consider how our online presence can help ourselves and others direct our thoughts to what is noble and just. And perhaps what we share can inspire social change or personal conversions.

If your fast does not include complete withdrawal from social media, share some good news through your posts today. If you refrain from all social media use during your fast, then consider how you can act with justice, prudence, temperance, and courage in your interactions with others in real life.

*Christ Jesus, teacher of a life of virtue, help me to live my online life with respect for others, using my media to build up the community and to offer hope and light to a world often wrapped in darkness.*

*WEEK 2 TUESDAY*

# Demythologizing Porn

Do you not know that your body is a temple of the Holy Spirit within you, which you have from God, and that you are not your own? For you were bought with a price; therefore glorify God in your body.

*—1 Corinthians 6:19–20*

It's no secret that porn is global mainstream entertainment. It is a multi-billion-dollar industry, with billions of views monthly.[13] Some of the most popular porn sites get more regular online traffic per month than most social media sites combined. Even though porn has historically been seen as a problem for men, it is increasingly an issue for women as well. And young people, especially children, are exposed to it online at an early age.[14] Porn is so prevalent that one survey shows that most young adults are encouraging, accepting, or neutral when talking about porn with friends.[15]

But what is pornography doing to us as human beings? Professor and researcher Gary Wilson explains the science related to adverse effects of porn on the brain, such as the inability to concentrate, loss of attraction to real life partners, desire for endless novelty, and depression, to name a few.[16] How is porn affecting our relationships and our society as a whole? Sex abuse, human trafficking, and abortion are all linked to growth of the porn industry.[17]

This media fast helps us to address the unhealthy ways we use particular types of media and why. If porn has been a struggle for you, this fast is an opportunity to pay closer attention to when you are experiencing cravings and to evaluate why you turn to pornography. Porn is often engaged with out of curiosity, or because "everyone's doing it." Other causes may be a need for affirmation, a desire to be loved or pursued, or an effort to escape and numb uncomfortable emotions. But porn can also become a sinful habit or an addiction. Using pornography harms the user and creator since it demeans everyone who is involved in producing and consuming it. Whatever the situation, porn enslaves us to our passions, drawing us away from the pure, self-giving love for which God created sex.

The body is sacred, "a temple of the Holy Spirit," Saint Paul informs the Corinthians. When respected and reverenced, the body gives glory to the creator. Porn destroys our ability to recognize the sacredness of the body by turning it into an object for pleasure. It dismembers the human being instead of portraying the whole person with emotions and personality. In his "Theology of the Body," Saint John Paul II explains that God creates human beings for love—a love that is generative and creative.

Practicing the virtues of purity, temperance, and prudence can help us avoid or free ourselves from the influence of porn. Saint John Paul II affirms that purity is centered on respect for the body through modesty and awareness of the gift of the Holy Spirit within us.[18] Similarly, the related virtue of chastity tempers the passions through self-mastery and "maintains the integrity of the powers of life and love"[19] in each person. We cultivate these virtues by being attentive to our reactions to media that depict sexually arousing content, by choosing to remove media that tempt us to commit sexual sin, and by praying for help to master our passions. The more we choose to act virtuously, the more we will move toward living "the good life" in Christ.

---

If pornography is a struggle for you, then use your time during this fast to work on changing your habits. Rather than trying to meet your needs with porn use, allow Jesus to be the one who affirms, pursues, and loves you. These changes require discernment and sometimes expert guidance. Talking to a priest-confessor in the sacrament of Reconciliation can be a good place to start. If necessary, you can also seek professional help to guide you to freedom from addiction (see Appendix B, page 201).

*Jesus, you know the challenges I face with the accessibility of pornography. Help me to turn my mind and heart to you when I feel tempted to disrespect the gift of my body and those of others.*

# Online Be-Attitudes

I hereby command you: Be strong and courageous; do not be frightened or dismayed, for the Lord your God is with you wherever you go.

*—Joshua 1:9*

MORE THAN 40 PERCENT of adults experience online harassment.[20] Harassment emerges in the form of sexual provocation, stalking, derisive or belittling comments, or cyberbullying. We may encounter online harassment directed at ourselves or at others. In one incident, a college student made it into a top law school while a fellow student did not. Out of jealousy, the other student posted derogatory remarks about her on a site populated by trolls. Soon sexualized comments and threats directed at her began to spread online.

When we encounter such situations, how do we respond? Even though the law student suffered from the harassment, she courageously channeled her experience into legal expertise to help others in similar situations. Instead of responding in anger, she took the path of prudence and temperance, enabling other victims of online harassment to receive justice.

Jesus invites his disciples to respond with virtue as he himself did when faced with harassment or ridicule. Saint Thomas Aquinas states that the virtue of courage gives strength of will to consistently practice virtue. Courage or fortitude is the willingness to choose what is right in the face of fear or obstacles. Virtuous engagement with media calls for continual application of the virtues of prudence, justice, temperance, and courage in all our entertainment and social engagements, especially when addressing situations that leave us "frightened or dismayed," as Scripture says.

These virtues help us to grow in our reliance on God through our online experiences and to act as authentic disciples of Christ. They are the *Be-Attitudes of Social Media* and challenge us to:

~ *Be prudent* in what we post, snap, or like; and consider sharing what helps us and others to live "a good life."

~ *Be just* in our posts by seeking out the truth in honesty and goodness, remembering there are always two sides to a story.

~ *Be temperate* in our media use, choosing well how to spend our time.

~ *Be courageous* by speaking the truth in charity and defending those who are being bullied.

Today, pray about how to incorporate these virtues, the Be-Attitudes, into your daily online engagement. How can you be prudent, just, temperate, and courageous online? What needs to change in you so you can be a virtuous witness of Christ in your media?

*Christ our Master, fill my heart with courage, prudence, justice, and temperance as I engage with my media. May I be your witness in the face of persecution, always offering love and respect even when the opposite is shown to me. I know you are with me.*

# The Lasso Effect

"Do not judge, so that you may not be judged. For with the judgment you make you will be judged, and the measure you give will be the measure you get."

—*Matthew 7:1–2*

IN THE COMEDY SERIES *Ted Lasso,* Jason Sudeikis stars as an optimistic and others-centered soccer coach. Once a small-time American football coach from Kansas, Ted becomes the head coach of the Premier League British soccer team, AFC Richmond. He knows nothing about soccer. But what he does know is that virtue matters, and most importantly, people matter. His care and concern for others, his hope and belief, become the hallmarks of his character. Though the show and Ted's character are not without flaws, Ted exudes virtues that support "the good life."

Conflict in media tends to hold our attention. Among the conflict-ridden shows and other media forms, Ted's agreeable character stands out. He reveals the beauty of positivity and likability and so challenges us to be better. Instead of being bothered by others' negative reactions toward him, Ted responds to conflict by saying: "Be curious. Not judgmental."[21]

Jesus adds a challenging twist when he says that if you judge others, you will be judged. Instead, being curious, kind, and merciful broadens our hearts. Ted Lasso reflects that all the people who criticized him lacked curiosity and judged everyone. He says, "I realized that their underestimating me—who I was had nothing to do with it. Because if they were curious, they would've asked questions."[22] Ted gets the Gospel maxim.

The internet is not always the best place to engage in deep debate. Sometimes calm and reasoned exchanges online can create respectful understanding, but when possible, it's better to have conversations about complex topics in person. Being able to see the other person's nonverbal communication provides greater understanding than simply reading words on a screen. But even if we only interact with someone online, we can remember that the other person is a real human being, not just the sum of his or her opinions. Keeping this in mind awakens curiosity and empathy, even if differences of opinion still remain when the conversation ends.

Fasting from our media may include not only limiting access, but also considering what and how we choose to post and interact with others' comments. Fasting challenges us to be mindful followers of Jesus, who urges us to love without judgment. Regardless of the insults we may receive, we are called to be kind even when the other remains an enemy.

————————⦿————————

What is your reaction when someone online responds to your post with offensive words? Do you react in anger and judgment? Today, consider how you can be curious without being judgmental.

*Jesus, you call me to love all people, including those I encounter online. Lead me to be your gentle and humble disciple who sows love amid judgment and peace when faced with conflict.*

# The Reality of Evil

For our struggle is not against enemies of blood and flesh,
but against the rulers, against the authorities, against the
cosmic powers of this present darkness, against the spiritual forces of evil in the heavenly places.

—*Ephesians 6:12*

ONCE I WAS ASKED to be on a panel for a *Horror and Christianity*
conference to talk about Catholic symbolism in horror films. It
surprised me how popular these movies are across all age groups.
Horror fans flock to them to experience the natural high of endor-
phins and adrenaline or to confront their fears. But in these movies
we also come face-to-face with the darkness within ourselves and
in the world. When our own fears seem overwhelming, movies
can be an outlet to express our deepest emotions. And some horror
films can make audiences aware of the presence of the devil when
many people today deny his existence.

The supernatural horror genre can influence the culture's moral imagination about the reality of evil. When movies and TV series show the devil as an evil being who can only be overcome by
good, as in William Friedkin's 1973 film *The Exorcist*, they affirm
that God is more powerful than Satan. Though many movies or
TV shows' representations of evil and of Catholic imagery are not
accurate, they still promote thoughtful questioning about issues of
faith and spirituality. The use of Catholic sacraments and sacra-
mentals, such as the Eucharist, the rosary, and the crucifix, alludes
to the mystery of faith and the power of good over evil.

Other horror films and TV series' plots dabble with the devil
without any clear direction about how to overcome supernatural

evil. They spiral into dangerous territory when portraying possession by evil spirits as a game. Without acknowledgment of a greater supernatural power for good, some storytelling media nihilistically conclude that evil reigns, without ever showing any power greater than evil. Though objects and activities like Ouija boards and séances may be portrayed by the media as inconsequential, they open participants to the devil's influence, which can lead to demonic obsession (influence from outside the person) or possession (taking over a person from the inside). Sometimes people learn too late that the devil is real and more powerful than human beings. When we turn to sources of power other than Christ, the devil steps in.

As we evaluate what it means to live virtuously with our media, we confront the choices we make that can open doors to the devil working on us or in us. Do we play occultic online games, or consult digital horoscopes or palm readers? Do we engage with entertainment media that present evil as good or isolate us from others? Do we seek healing of emotional wounds from sources that lead us away from God?

Saint Paul says we are constantly fighting "against the cosmic powers of this present darkness." The devil is powerful, but not invincible. God is more powerful than any evil. The most powerful antidotes to evil are the sacraments, especially the sacrament of Confession. Many exorcists say that a good confession is worth more than any exorcism. Rejecting the devil's influence in your life leads to accepting Christ as the center of your heart. With him you live "the good life."

———————o○o———————

During this fast, consider the reality of evil and sin in the world and in your own heart. Consider scheduling a time to go to the sacrament of Confession to experience the healing and transforming power of God over sin.

*Jesus, I turn to you for healing from the darkness that keeps me from you. I believe that evil has no power over me when I am united with you and your Mother Mary. Help me to see and witness to the mystery of faith that conquers all evil. In you, Lord, my fear turns to trust.*

*WEEK 2 SATURDAY*

# Hope in an Anxious World

> We also boast in our sufferings, knowing that suffering produces endurance, and endurance produces character, and character produces hope, and hope does not disappoint us, because God's love has been poured into our hearts through the Holy Spirit that has been given to us.
>
> —*Romans 5:3–5*

A MEDIA FAST REMOVES digital stressors from our lives and affords us time to assess our prayer lives and consider our mental health. We can also use the additional time to reflect on how to ground our hope in God, who alone gives hope to an anxious world.

During this week, we have focused specifically on the cardinal virtues of courage, prudence, justice, and temperance. We conclude with a reflection on one of the theological virtues—hope. Hope gives us the motivation to keep moving forward and sustains us in the truth that Jesus will always be with us even when darkness and discouragement cloud our vision of life. When the world comes crashing down upon us, our belief in Jesus is our anchor of hope through the storms.

As part of the Daughters of St Paul's "Scripture Minute" series, I recorded a sixty-second reflection about appreciating the gifts God has given us instead of hiding our talents in fear. The culmination of this reflection was finding hope in the struggles of life. One person commented on Instagram: "Wow! It's as if this message was timed just perfectly to speak to my heart." The commenter noted that fear and self-doubt prevent us from authentically reaching out to others in love and drag down our spirits, while appreciating God's gifts opens us to selflessness and brings hope to the world. One video made a difference for someone struggling to find hope and meaning in life.

Perhaps we feel the need to pray for the virtue of hope for ourselves and for others who are discouraged by life's challenges. The Lord helps us see that it is not only the grand gestures of life that matter, but the small, daily choices for good. These are the moments in which we practice virtue and help people to recognize hope in their own lives. Saint Paul assures us, "suffering produces endurance, and endurance produces character, and character produces hope, and hope does not disappoint us." Sharing grace-filled moments in an authentic way through our media, without ignoring the difficulties of life, proves what Saint Paul says. Discovering something positive in our suffering helps us endure the pain but also illustrates to others that there is always hope because Christ redeems our suffering through his glorious resurrection. The end is not death, but life!

How can we use our media to bring hope into someone else's life? We can start by using our media prayerfully. I often ask the Lord: *Please help me bring a little light and joy into the world today.* If I do nothing else in life but leave the world a better place than it is right now, then God has answered that prayer. To respond with a blessing to those who air out their frustrations on our feed, or to make a reel of one grace we received that day, can be ways of offering hope to the world.

Ask yourself: *What can I do to bring a little light and hope to another person online?* Ask the Lord for his grace to respond and to be his instrument of hope in an anxious world.

*Jesus, you desire my good and show me a future of hope with you. Give me the grace to keep my gaze on you and to be your instrument of hope to an anxious, ailing world.*

# Media Fast Check-in

How's your media fast going? What was your most significant fasting experience this week? Did you feel tempted to break your fast? What helped you keep the fast or return to it after you halted?

## Prayer in Reparation for the Misuse of the Media

*Jesus, I pray now especially for the conversion of all those creative media artists and technicians who use their talents to spread divisiveness, disinformation, and morally harmful entertainment that demeans the human person and leads others to sin. May my daily media choices for good break the cycle of harm and allow your Holy Spirit to infiltrate the culture with your truth, beauty, and goodness. Amen.*

## You Can Do This

Growing in virtue is a lifelong process that involves one step at a time, trusting in the goodness and mercy of God. We won't be perfectly virtuous all at once, but we can keep moving forward one choice at a time toward our goal of living "the good life" in Christ.

The only defeat in life is to yield to difficulty, to abandon the struggle.[23]

—Blessed James Alberione

## Life Hack for the Week

Use this acronym to practice virtue in your media use:

T.H.I.N.K. Before sharing something online or through other media, consider:

T = Is it true?

H = Is it helpful?

I  = Is it inspiring?

N = Is it necessary?

K = Is it kind?

# WEEK 3

# Being Media Mindful

[The media] have powerful influence on the masses. They can gravely undermine or greatly reinforce the four hinges of human life: the family, the social order, the religious order, the human-moral order.[24]

—*Blessed James Alberione*

I HAD THE OPPORTUNITY to be a contestant on a pilot episode of a reality baking show. Though I'm not an expert baker, the director convinced me to show up for filming because the producers really wanted a nun-contestant. It took three days, and we often filmed late into the night before the episode would wrap. Even though the other contestants and I were there to bake, so much on the set was scripted. The showrunners were constantly coming to me giving me lines to say or something specific to do. As a nun, I guess I was the novelty on set and added the entertainment factor! Unfortunately, the show was never aired, but the experience showed me that all media are constructed, even reality TV.

Our fast includes learning to be mindful of the media we consume. This means we become conscious of the media's messages and how they are constructed. This is a key element of media literacy, which is the ability to access, evaluate, analyze, and create media messages. Being media mindful integrates media literacy skills with our faith, so that our choices about what we engage with will be based on our beliefs. Media mindfulness teaches us to ask questions of the media and bring our faith values into dialogue with media messages.

The more media mindful we are, the more we reflect on all that we see, hear, and feel when we engage with our media. A principle of media literacy is that all media are constructed. That is, they are created through a process of choices by the artists, filmmakers, designers, authors, or editors, using specific techniques to grab our attention. All media present specific points of view and values. Even reality shows are scripted according to the desired outcome of the producers.

By examining structure and storytelling techniques, we gain a better idea of how a show or other form of media is made and why. Yet that is only one part of being media literate. The crucial part is asking questions: *Why is this message being sent? What values, ideologies, lifestyles, or points of view are being communicated?* For Christians, Gospel values and the example of Jesus guide our interaction with those messages and inform our media use.

## Media Mindfulness How-to

As a film and TV reviewer, I watch movies and streaming shows and reflect on the theology present in the popular culture. I also regularly consider how to integrate a reflective, spiritual life with all the media we use and create. The many different shows and forms of media present messages that need careful discernment, so I work on developing the skill of media mindfulness and help others to do the same.

Some television shows and other forms of media, though not perfect, can serve to inspire and uplift. Some need more thoughtful, questioning approaches because of the way they deal with particular issues or resolve the moral situations presented. Then there is media content that portrays an amoral view of life, placing all behaviors on the same moral playing field or promoting agendas directly opposed to human dignity and Christian morality. Because of the abundance of media options and the reality that not all content reflects Christian values, media mindfulness is a crucial skill for our digital age. It's a learned practice that requires making sacrifices and conscious choices for the good.

The media mindfulness wheel helps us to go deeper as we ask critical questions of the media experience.[25]

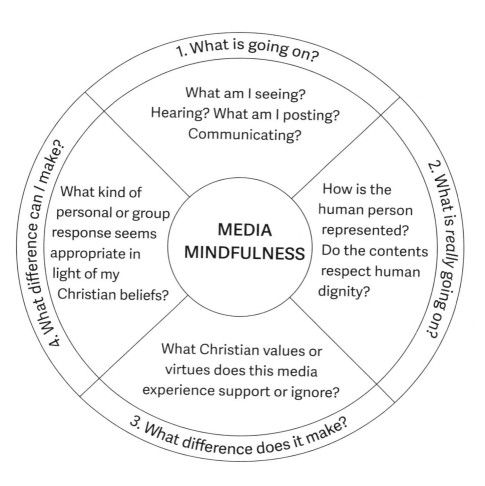

# Choosing Media Wisely

Even if we remove some or all of our media for a specified period during our fast, we may resume using it when the fast ends. Therefore, it's crucial to use this time of fasting to develop the skill of media mindfulness and to incorporate this skill into our fasting plan.

Like our fasting plan, media mindfulness is a way of holding ourselves accountable for what we watch, read, engage with, or listen to. We can use this practice for streaming shows, movies, news, podcasts, music, video games, social media posts, and other forms of media. Media mindfulness helps us determine whether certain media messages support Christian and human values, whether we personally should engage with such media, and how we can respond to the messages presented. Mindfulness teaches us to become critical thinkers, not passive absorbers of the culture's ideologies.

For example, video games with intense violent action can sometimes influence our thoughts and feelings. Watching a movie with indiscriminate killing can desensitize us to actual violence. At the same time, killing a character in a video game is not the same as killing someone in real life, nor does witnessing murder in a television show make watching that show an automatically bad moral choice. When we see an onscreen character exhibit immoral behavior or play a game that allows or necessitates bad choices, it does not mean that we condone the action. We can take what is good and leave the rest. However, if something is directly opposed to our Christian values and has the potential to be harmful to our souls over time—for example, if a show portrays soft porn or if a video game makes the user perpetrate torture on another—we may need to discern whether to continue to engage with it. We also should take into account our own personal sensitivities and circumstances when it comes to viewing trauma or dark, twisted portrayals of evil. We should make sure that the media we use don't prevent us from living out the Gospel values that Jesus teaches us.

As Christians, we are to live our faith in the concrete experiences of our lives, and that includes our media experience. Media mindfulness benefits our overall media use by helping us evaluate media messages according to our faith and make choices that support our well-being of body and soul. Our fast can be a good time to start practicing media mindfulness, so that it will become a habit to help us live well with our media and support the health of our whole being.

*WEEK 3 SUNDAY*

# Our Music Canon

My heart is steadfast, O God,
      my heart is steadfast.
I will sing and make melody.

*—Psalm 57:7*

WHAT DO OUR MUSIC playlists say about us?

I listen to all different genres of music depending on my mood or interest. I move from alternative to pop, hip-hop to blues, classic rock to country. The creativity of artists who develop new musical expressions and soul-stirring lyrics enthralls me. Some people like me listen to a wide variety of music styles. Others enjoy one genre and the many musicians within that category. Whatever music fills your playlist, you can "sing and make melody," as the Psalmist says.

Music often comes to us digitally and so may be part of our digital media fast. If music is not part of our fast, we can still take this time to reflect on the sounds and lyrics of the songs we most enjoy. How do we live mindful of our music?

Music can lead us to reflect on our relationships. Or it can have a great beat that makes us want to dance and have a good time. It can also raise our awareness of various issues that lead to social change. On the other hand, music can affect us negatively. Excessively violent lyrics or discordant sounds can disturb our souls or influence our behaviors. Explicit sexual lyrics can arouse our passions and provoke lustful urgings. Some music dwells on darkness so that the listener becomes desensitized to evil. Repeatedly exposing ourselves to these influences can lower our mood and affect how we think and feel.

Have we considered *why* we listen to the music we do? Are we mindful of the sounds and lyrics on our playlists? Awareness is how we begin to discern what songs we choose to listen to. Growing in understanding of music's powerful influence can help us make choices that support our mental, emotional, and spiritual well-being.

Considering all that you have reflected on so far during this fast, evaluate your music canon. Consider the lyrics and melody of one song and what Christian values it supports or ignores. Also reflect on how the song affects your emotions and thoughts. Based on this reflection, determine whether that song will remain on your playlist.

*God, Divine Artist, thank you for the gift of music that speaks deeply to my soul. Guide me to be mindful of the lyrics and sounds on my playlist, so that I may be better able to enjoy this precious gift that you have given for my enjoyment.*

*Week 3 Monday*

# Binge-Watching

For this very reason, you must make every effort to support your faith with goodness, and goodness with knowledge, and knowledge with self-control, and self-control with endurance, and endurance with godliness, and godliness with mutual affection, and mutual affection with love.

*—2 Peter 1:5–7*

I WAS ON A coast-to-coast Christmas concert tour when a season of *The Crown* dropped. Another sister and I were in the airport scrambling for free Wi-Fi access to download the latest episodes before boarding our connecting flight. It was a great way of passing time in the air. The drama surrounding the royal family captured the imagination of millions, including us nuns!

Bingeing a television series, Instagram reels, TikTok videos, music videos, or web comics can be irresistible. The characters in stories come alive, and we connect emotionally with their life circumstances. We want to find out what comes next and so we binge-watch the episodes or read the series over a very brief period. Short-form videos are often so attention-grabbing that we don't realize how much time we're spending with them. If this becomes our *modus operandi*, we may have to examine how we use our time. If bingeing cuts into our needed sleep, work, prayer, or in-person social time, it's a sign we need to reassess.

Evaluating the time we spend with our media develops our mindfulness strategy. When a new series became available, I decided to watch it with someone else and limit our viewing to one episode a night. This enabled us to talk about it together, which made the experience communal rather than individual. Talking about it afterward also helped us evaluate the messages of the show and how these did or did not align with our faith values.

In our Scripture today, Saint Peter says faith involves knowledge, goodness, and self-control. Media mindfulness, like media fasting, is about self-control. When a favorite series posts a new season, the plots are so intriguing and addictive that we just want to watch the whole series at once to find out the ending. Self-control makes us conscious of our viewing time. Watching just one episode a night of our favorite series keeps us wanting more without overindulging our curiosity and helps us grow in discipline, an essential element to faith.

One way to keep yourself accountable is to use the media mindfulness wheel, especially the third part. Doing this helps you to evaluate messages and how much time you spend watching TV and streaming shows. Ask yourself: *What Christian values, virtues, social issues does this support or ignore?* Then ask: *What am I getting out of this content? Does it help me reflect on some aspect of life or relationships? Does it help me grow in virtue? How much time am I spending on this show?*

*Master of my heart, let me indulge only in your love for me and in giving love through kindness and goodness to others. Keep me from excess in using media so my mind and heart can be awake and attentive to my daily prayer and tasks.*

*WEEK 3 TUESDAY*

# Is Google the New God?

Happy are those who find wisdom,
　　and those who get understanding,
for her income is better than silver,
　　and her revenue better than gold.
She is more precious than jewels,
　　and nothing you desire can compare with her.

*—Proverbs 3:13–15*

WHERE DO YOU TURN when you struggle? When you need help? When you have a heavy burden and need to relieve the weight from your soul?

In the pre-digital age, people burdened by dark secrets or desperate to discover life's answers turned to friends, family, or God. The internet has changed the way we seek advice. Moreover, it's often where we turn to seek answers to life's problems.

Google, the largest search engine in the world, fills up with queries about everyday problems. How do I restore lost data? Where is the nearest coffee shop? Who has the best pizza in town? People also turn to the internet to seek answers about the meaning of life, how to be happy, how to deal with loneliness, and how to decide one's life path. Hoping to receive an answer we trust, we start scrolling through the one billion website results that appear in less than a second. Google has become the culture's savior.

If Google is our god, what role does Jesus play in our lives? When confusion fills our minds and our souls hurt, do we peer into a screen? When sin or sorrow scar our hearts, do we turn to Google to find answers to or distraction from our suffering? If the internet becomes our place of refuge, we may find loneliness and pain instead of an answer we trust. We can confuse information with wisdom.

Jesus intimately knows our sufferings and all that is in our hearts. As the Book of Proverbs says, "Happy are those who find wisdom and those who get understanding." Jesus alone gives us what we truly need. Deeply acquainted with suffering, he knows what it means to be human and understands our pains, hopes, and desires, something an inanimate search engine can never do. Google provides information. Jesus provides wisdom.

Reflect on where you seek truth or the answers to life's fundamental questions. Bring one of those questions to God in prayer today.

*Jesus, you are the Truth for which we long. Be the knowledge that I seek and guide me in my search for true wisdom beyond what Google can provide. You alone are my Savior and Redeemer. May everything I seek lead me to you, my Way, my Truth, and my Life.*

# Discerning Ideologies

Proclaim the message; be persistent whether the time is favorable or unfavorable; convince, rebuke, and encourage, with the utmost patience in teaching. For the time is coming when people will not put up with sound doctrine, but having itching ears, they will accumulate for themselves teachers to suit their own desires, and will turn away from listening to the truth and wander away to myths. As for you, always be sober, endure suffering, do the work of an evangelist, carry out your ministry fully.

*—2 Timothy 4:2–5*

POLITICS SHOW UP IN almost everything we do, especially when media platforms allow us to share our thoughts and ideas. News outlets present various worldviews. Entertainment media transmit values within the stories, fantasies, or comedic situations they portray. Each of us has a particular point of view on laws, morals, and human living, but so do media outlets, corporations, and governments. These points of view are sets of beliefs and opinions known as ideologies. Ideologies are systems of ideas meant to influence a populace. They are not neutral, but are often tied to political ends, such as communism, capitalism, socialism, liberalism, and conservatism. Others, such as gender ideologies, are more social or cultural in nature but can also be intertwined with political motives.

Ideologies and religions both deal with truths and conduct, but they are quite different. Religion centers on divine order, whereas ideologies focus on this world alone.[26] When we seek the meaning of our life in ideological worldviews, they become our guiding force, but they can never truly fulfill us, since we are made for more than this world. When we seek Christ, love for God and the truth of the human person become our guiding principles. Jesus teaches us about the truths of human dignity, moral choices that respect each human being, and the law of love. Politics are fickle. Christ's law is eternal. And that's worth staking our lives on!

Ideologies in the culture require us to constantly ask questions of every movie, TV series, social post, and news coverage. News is especially politicized and most news outlets exhibit certain biases. Social media algorithms keep us in news bubbles that validate existing beliefs rather than reveal different perspectives. Practicing media mindfulness with reported news becomes crucial for discovering the truth. Sometimes it's helpful to read about the same event from several sources with differing political views. This can offer a more complete picture of the story from various angles. Distinguishing news sources' biases can lead us to find outlets that are more "balanced" in their reporting. This helps us to engage thoughtfully with the media instead of reacting rashly.

Media mindfulness also helps us determine the compatibility of the various ideologies within the media with our beliefs about human freedom and dignity. As Paul warns Timothy, we don't follow ideologies. We follow Jesus Christ. He is the measure of all truth. Paul encourages Timothy, and us, to be "sober"—that is, to be attentive and make sure we measure the ideologies we encounter against our faith, rather than allow ourselves to be led by them.

Practice media mindfulness with today's news stories. If your fast includes abstaining from reading news or political commentaries, then practice this critical inquiry with one other media experience.

*Jesus Truth, the influence of the various political ideologies can be overwhelming. Sometimes it's hard to discern what's true. Show me yourself as the Truth on which I can stake my life. You alone are the treasure that gives my life meaning.*

*WEEK 3 THURSDAY*

# Gender Disinformation

So God created humankind in his image,
 in the image of God he created them;
 male and female he created them.

*— Genesis 1:27*

THE POPULAR MEDIA CULTURE assents to the growing acceptance of gender ideology, a theory that one's inner sense of gender determines one's identity as a woman or man even if this does not correspond to one's biological sex. It's in video games, manga series, television, music, social media, film, and theater. TikTok alone amasses billions of views of transgender content under #trans. Some video games and other media amplify non-binary or gender fluid characters. The media culture advocates gender ideology as a means to finding one's identity as a path to happiness.

Many who experience gender dysphoria struggle with deep psychological wounds. The normalization of gender ideologies in storytelling and news may be intended to be compassionate, but it contributes to social contagion by adding to the confusion about what it means to be human, body and soul, male or female. Sometimes we may feel insecure because of social pressure caused by media promotion of gender ideologies, gender stereotypes we feel we must live up to, or idealized body types we see in media. But our true worth does not come from our emotions or external validation; it comes from our identity as a son or daughter of God. Even though emotional or psychological pain may lead us to question our gender, our whole being—physical and spiritual, body and soul—is created in God's image and likeness as a unique and unrepeatable gift. No hormone therapy, "gender-affirming" surgery, or pronoun will change our God-given sexual identity as woman or man. Seeking chemical and surgical interventions to relieve distress or express personal autonomy will not alleviate the deep psychological or emotional scars. We can't fix the soul by altering the body.

The human body possesses dignity as a temple of the Holy Spirit. It is an expression of beauty. Biological sex indicates a person's immutable male or female identity, present in each cell of the body. Trying to change this gift mars the wholeness of the human person, body and soul.

Through media mindfulness, we can examine how media represent the human person and recognize when these representations include biases that contradict the Church's teaching. Are human bodies depicted as objects we can change at will on the basis of feelings? How does a particular media message affect the way we see the human person and the Church's teachings? Is it compassionate to affirm persons in their error? The #transtok videos of gender reassignment surgeries only show one aspect of a person's life. Being mindful of the media's influence regarding gender ideology will help us integrate the Church's understanding of the human person into our response to what we listen to, watch, or read.

To be a disciple of Christ calls us to respect God's immutable gift through and in the media we use. We love and value every person, regardless of that person's struggles with gender. Each human being has been loved into existence by God and deserves respect because of that dignity. But love also means guiding others to discover the truth of their God-given identity. We can do this through online engagement or choices not to engage with media that promote or support gender ideologies.

Pray for all who struggle with gender identification. Reaching out with loving attention may be the way to support someone's discovery of their identity in Christ and the created beauty of each human being.

*Heavenly Father, the struggle for identity is real. Help me to find my identity in you as your child. Let me be your instrument of love and truth in a culture confused about what it means to be made in your image and likeness.*

*WEEK 3 FRIDAY*

# The Swiping Game

For surely I know the plans I have for you, says the Lord, plans for your welfare and not for harm, to give you a future with hope.

—*Jeremiah 29:11*

IN THE UNITED STATES, online dating has become the most common way to meet a romantic partner.[27] There are over 1500 dating apps with close to 400 million users worldwide.[28] Many of these apps focus on connecting people through a shared worldview or interest, including some Catholic dating apps, which help people connect with others who share their faith.

Many of these apps have led to lasting marriages. However, dating apps can also have negative effects. They may lead us to make comparisons and question our self-worth. Some people constantly swipe right to increase their desirability score, especially if they feel insecure about their chances of success. Being on an app for a while without finding a suitable match, or being rejected, can lead people to feel they aren't "successful" and to become discouraged or cynical. If we feel "unsuccessful" in relationships, we can remember that everything happens in God's time, not ours. God cares for each of us and will support us throughout our lives.

For such a momentous life experience, these apps with their swiping or matching options can make meeting people seem like a game. A dating app can reduce persons to their profile picture instead of encouraging us to take time to get to know them. But people are more complex than their online profiles. They are real human beings with feelings and personalities, hopes and dreams. Our online relationships deserve the same respect and sensitivity as our in-person relationships. The way we treat people we meet online matters whether we end up in a romantic relationship with them or not.

Applying media mindfulness skills to dating apps makes us realize that algorithms are fallible and cannot reveal all the amazing complexities of another person. When we recognize Christ in each person we interact with, then the person behind the profile becomes someone worthy of our respect. We afford them the dignity they deserve and the kindness that builds them up.

The perfect match is a God-given gift. And God can use technology or other means for two people to meet. Whether you use any dating apps or not, you can pray to grow in trust in God, believing he has a plan for you, "to give you a future with hope."

*Heavenly Father, help me to develop whole and healthy relationships with the people I meet online. Let me not be discouraged when I lack intimacy with others. Help me believe that everything will be revealed by you in time. Help me to trust that you know what is best for me.*

# Examination of My Online Life

Examine yourselves to see whether you are living in the
faith. Test yourselves. Do you not realize that Jesus Christ
is in you?

*—2 Corinthians 13:5*

THE INSTANTANEOUS NATURE OF our media culture leaves little
room for reflection. When I read a passionate controversial social
media post that I disagree with, my impulsive response is to want
to "correct" the person's way of thinking. It takes me a conscious
moment of reflection to realize that I'm not going to change someone's mind and that my "correcting" response could imply anger or
a lack of charity. Generally, this type of conversation isn't bene-
ficial when mediated through a screen. In such circumstances, I
often conclude that the best response is no response. Without that
moment of reflective pause, things could become verbally volatile.

Self-reflection is the ability to become aware of and evaluate
our own emotions, ideas, and behaviors. It takes practice to question ourselves so as to make choices that align with our values of
love of God and love of neighbor.

A helpful spiritual practice for growing in reflection is the examination of conscience. This is the process of prayerfully looking
at ourselves to consider how our thoughts, words, and actions may
have hurt our relationships with God and others. Examining ourselves daily is an important aspect of fasting as we reflect on how
we behave when using our media. This spiritual practice holds us
accountable for our actions and helps us to change unruly habits.

Making an examination of conscience specifically on our online experience leads us to become media mindful by helping us

see how we act in and through our media and how we choose to engage with media that are helpful or harmful to our soul. Examining our conscience daily can truly change our life, since it leads us to greater self-reflection. When we examine our behavior, we are more apt to change our habits because we pay more attention to what is happening in our soul. We confront our life with the life of Christ, our actions with his actions, our desires with his desires. When we reflect on how to become more Christ-like, opening our heart to learn from the Lord, he presents himself to us. The more we become the best version of ourself, the more Christ will shine in and through us.

Take some moments of reflection today using the *Examination of Conscience for My Online Life* (see Appendix D). You can make this a daily or weekly spiritual practice by setting aside ten minutes to use this guide.

*Heavenly Father, thank you for knowing me more than I know myself. I recognize that the way I use media sometimes leads me or others away from you. Help me not to abuse these technological gifts, but instead to use them for your glory and others' good. Forgive me for my failings and help me to be the best version of myself.*

# Media Fast Check-in

Look again at your fasting plan and the list of triggers that lead you to problematic media usage. Are they still triggers for you, or have they changed? Have you noticed any new triggers?

## Prayer in Reparation for the Misuse of the Media

*Jesus, my Divine Savior, I offer you my efforts to be your digital witness, in union with your sacrifice celebrated on all the altars throughout the world, in atonement for all persons who misuse the media. I promise to always use media for my own growth in holiness and to communicate your saving Word with creativity and joy. Amen.*

## You Can Do This

Examining our behaviors and the messages we consume is the heart of media mindfulness. Let's be aware of our media consumption while seeking union with God.

> Let us examine calmly what good, what evil, and what fruits there might be; then let us get busy doing good and taking away abuses.[29]

> —Blessed James Alberione

## Life Hack for the Week

Place your phone on the opposite side of the room from your bed so you won't look at it before going to sleep and must get up to turn off the alarm in the morning.

# WEEK 4

# Becoming Cultural Mystics

When the means of progress serve evangelization, a consecration takes place, and they are elevated to the fullest dignity. The writer's office, the technician's plant . . . become a church and pulpit. The one who works in them rises to the dignity of an apostle.[30]

*—Blessed James Alberione*

WE OFTEN SEE PEOPLE struggle to fill an interior emptiness, to satisfy that bottomless hunger for something more than what this world offers. Sometimes we may feel that longing ourselves. Current trends that seek to address the spiritual yearnings of the human person garner attention in the media. Some of those trends involve mysticism. Mysticism is often popularly understood as absorption into a deity or altered states of consciousness given a spiritual meaning. Many people seek out this type of mysticism in crystals and tarot cards or manifestation affirmations, a technique to turn positive thinking into a reality or to see into the future. However, these kinds of practices are problematic because they lead people to seek perfection and salvation in something other than God himself. Understood in this sense, mysticism can lead to superstition or immoral outcomes, as well as self-absorption and materialism with no view to life beyond the grave. More problematic are the occultic connections associated with these practices that can lead people to commune with demons.

Mysticism in the Christian tradition is a transformative experience of God in Christ. Delighting in a glorious mountain view, holding a newborn baby, or reflecting on a YouTube video that leads us to think of God can all elicit spiritual awareness. A mystical encounter, however, touches us at the core of our being and changes us. Encountering Christ in this way as the one who can fulfill all our deepest yearnings transforms us by captivating our whole being. Christ's beauty consumes us and we respond by converting our lives to become more like him. We no longer see and experience ourselves or the world in the same way. Our whole life focus shifts to revolve around our relationship with Christ. Through mystical union, Christ sets us free from the forces of evil and fulfills our most profound desires for love, acceptance, connection, purpose, and meaning. We bring a mystical encounter with God into our engagement of the popular media culture by looking at cultural stories with the eyes of faith.

## Cultural Mysticism

Each of us can be a *cultural mystic*,[31] a person who sees the existential desires of humanity in the trends of the popular media culture and seeks to present Christ as the answer to all those yearnings. Our transformative relationship with Christ influences how we understand the deep questionings present in the art of the culture and helps us to draw out the elements of grace. Cultural mystics view stories in the world of media through the lens of the sacred. They see God's grace at work in the secular culture because everything human is of interest to God. Jesus, God become man, sanctified and redeemed humanity by taking on flesh to show us what true humanity looks like. The yearnings often present in popular cultural artifacts are spiritual longings for the best of our human nature, which reflects elements of Christ's beauty, truth, and goodness.

The cultural mystic's journey follows Saint Paul's example. The Apostle lived his transforming relationship with Christ within the culture that surrounded him. He used the media of his day (letters) to communicate the love of God to people lost in confusion about what it means to be human, caught up in idolatry and perversion. From Paul we take our cue to be disciples who support human dignity, human freedom, and respect for each person as made in the image of God. Saint Paul's main concern was that people come to know Jesus. This meant that he had to address the needs and longings of the people of his time, using his voice and his pen to present Christ as the one, true, and only answer. His followers have taken up his style of mysticism to live as mystics in the world while proclaiming the Gospel of Jesus Christ to the culture of our day.

## Pauline Spirituality

Saint Paul's mysticism impassioned Blessed James Alberione's missionary spirit. As founder of the Pauline Family—ten religious institutes evangelizing the culture in and through media—Alberione was the first to express and live the Pauline media spirituality. He described it as allowing Christ to live in us by following Saint Paul's example of communicating the transforming power of Christ's life. And for Alberione, that meant doing so through all forms of media. At his beatification, Saint John Paul II called Alberione the "Apostle of the New Evangelization," a true media apostle.

Communicating the Gospel message within the media culture, seeking to address the yearnings of humanity, is the heart of a media spirituality. Alberione reflects that a mystic's heart "needs to be more vast than the seas and the oceans."[32] He proposes that we become imbued with Christ through his Word and Eucharist—the Bible and the Blessed Sacrament. The heart of the cultural mystic is formed by learning the Truth from the Word who is Christ, spending time with the Lord in the Eucharist, receiving him into our being in Communion, and contemplating the needs of humanity. Then we are sent out as evangelizers of the Word in a culture that uses technology to communicate. The Pauline media spirituality, therefore, forms us to be cultural mystics who pray with the media we engage.

## Praying the Media

Praying the media means coming to know and understand God better by praying with and about our media experience. We look at what the media communicate, what existential desires they express, and how the Holy Spirit uses these to speak to us about our own lives. We pray with films, television series, video games, news stories, social media, books, and music. We find God's grace in the art of the culture by noticing what media communicate about the struggles and joys of human living.

We also pray for everyone working in the media—the creators, artists, programmers, directors, producers, and distributors. They are the culture-creators who have a responsibility to communicate the true, the good, and the beautiful. We pray that they may recognize their responsibility to tell stories that uphold human dignity and challenge us to recognize our need for redemption.

The more we delve into our relationship with Christ during this media fast, the more we will begin to see the world and the popular culture through the eyes of Christ. When we do so, we will recognize our own existential desires manifested in the stories and expressions of the media. We can then bring those into dialogue with our faith in Christ, who is the only Redeemer of humanity and the fulfillment of all our yearnings. Fasting helps us grow in cultural mysticism and so live our relationship with Christ long after the fast is over.

WEEK 4 SUNDAY

# Praying the News

"For God so loved the world that he gave his only Son, so that everyone who believes in him may not perish but may have eternal life. Indeed, God did not send the Son into the world to condemn the world, but in order that the world might be saved through him."

*—John 3:16–17*

MAJOR NEWS OUTLETS OFTEN get their breaking news from eyewitnesses who use their phones to capture live events. We see images of wildfires ripping through forests and buildings as people evacuate. We watch political protests, wars, and sometimes violent clashes of ideologies. Victims document earthquakes and tsunamis as they devastate coastal countries. When tragedy occurs anywhere around the globe, we receive instant news. Promises of prayer and solidarity go up on social media, uniting us with those who are most affected. Sometimes, though, all these tragedies bring us to the point of "doomscrolling," where we obsessively read every story related to the event and succumb to feelings of despair. Or we argue with others over the best way to respond to an incident and become more divided instead of united.

In the Gospel of John we read, "God did not send the Son into the world to condemn the world, but in order that the world might be saved through him." We find solace in the assurance that no matter what happens, our Heavenly Father, he who gave his Son for our salvation, is with us. When we pray with trust, we proclaim our faith in this eternal truth and surrender the needs of the world into his care. God wants us to trust that he cares for his people and seeks the good of all. We may see only the tragedy, but we do not know what miracles God is performing within the chaos and conflict.

Praying about current news events in our world directs our attention toward the needs of humanity. In times when fear and worry can turn us in on ourselves or make us turn against one another, praying about a situation and for the persons in it keeps the focus outside of ourselves. It can lead us to act on behalf of those affected by such tragedies, as well as to concentrate more on God and his promises. Prayer leads us to trust in God. Learning to pray the media is an important part of our media fast. Fasting is not only doing without our media for a period of time: it is especially attuning our hearts and minds to God and the needs of the world.

The practice of praying the news (see Appendix D) allows you to cope with world events peacefully, trusting in God. You can do this prayer by yourself or with a group.

*Heavenly Father, as I read or listen to the news, I bring before you all the needs of the world today. Help those who suffer, comfort those who are fearful, and bless those who make us smile. I trust in you and ask your intercession for everyone, especially all who are suffering.*

## WEEK 4 MONDAY

# Praying for Media Creators

"So I tell you, whatever you ask for in prayer, believe that
you have received it, and it will be yours."

—*Mark 11:24*

HAVE YOU EVER STAYED to watch all the credits after a movie
finishes? It takes an army of people to create just one two-hour
movie. I have had the opportunity to be present on the live film
and television sets of several Hollywood studios. The number of
talented artists and hardworking technicians behind the scenes is
astounding. Each one plays a part in the whole. When I talk to
makeup artists, wardrobe assistants, grips, showrunners, and celebrities, I make sure to tell them that I pray for them. They are always
so appreciative that someone thinks of them in that way.

All artists and media creators use their craft to tell stories and
express their personal depth through their art. Their creations have
the potential to uplift humanity and support human dignity. Because of how much their work influences the culture, these artists
and technicians need our prayers.

I've known the actor Jonathan Roumie for several years. As
the star of the popular series *The Chosen*, about the life of Jesus, he
has become a worldwide social influencer. We Daughters of St.
Paul pray for everyone working in media, and I remember telling
Jonathan when he was seeking work in Hollywood that we were
praying for him and that God would manifest his will at the right
time. A humble and faith-filled person, Jonathan appreciated the
prayers. Now that his creative influence touches millions of people
around the globe, I pray for him even more and tell him so when

I see him. It's not easy playing the part of Jesus, especially when people try to confess their sins to him!

Our fast can include intercessory prayers for specific culture-creators, or we can offer up some sacrifice—such as abstaining from technology we enjoy—to intercede for those who work in the media and entertainment industries. Praying a Rosary for their intentions can be another way to seek help for the creators of our media culture. In our prayers, we can ask that they create technology and entertainment for the betterment of humanity.

We are also media creators when we tell stories, share information, and supply content through media. This means that when we pray for all media creators, we are also praying for ourselves! We all have a responsibility to communicate what helps people reflect deeply on our common human experience and what uplifts others' spirits. When we do, our media creation reflects God, the Creator of all that is good.

Consider praying the Canticle of Praise for the Media (see Appendix C) today, asking that media creators may be light in the darkness. As Jesus says in Mark's Gospel, "Whatever you ask for in prayer . . . will be yours."

*Jesus, I pray for all those who create the popular media I consume daily. May they recognize their responsibility to build up the human family and communicate all that is true, good, and beautiful.*

*WEEK 4 TUESDAY*

# *Cinema Divina*

The Lord is near to all who call on him,
　　to all who call on him in truth.
He fulfills the desire of all who fear him;
　　he also hears their cry, and saves them.

*—Psalm 145:18–19*

AMERICAN ACTOR, DIRECTOR, AND producer Forest Whitaker once said, "Cinema and the arts invite viewers to focus on a story, and in doing so, peel away its layers and peer into the depths of the human soul."[33]

Visual stories—such as movies, television series, and video games—tell us about life. They reflect our common human experience, sometimes in outlandish and extraordinary ways. Every genre—sci-fi, drama, comedy, biopic, fantasy, action-adventure, thriller, horror—tells us something about what it means to be human. Visual stories bring characters to life through the classic plotline of action, background, conflict, development, and resolution. They often include a crisis point with consequences. This cultural form of storytelling embodies humanity's search for what is beyond the material universe.

Visual stories provide the space to reflect upon the existential desires we may not normally consider, such as our need for communion, connection, or meaning. They offer an opportunity to ponder our relationships and to address our deepest fears and our hopes for the future. Because cinema and other forms of visual storytelling have the power to lead us to consider the ultimate questions of life and direct us to the supernatural, they can be the catalyst for prayer and reflection on our relationship with God.

"He fulfills the desire of all who fear him," as the Psalmist says. Praying with visual stories can be a powerful tool in our spiritual lives.

What do our favorite stories say about our experience and the way we relate to the world, to one another, and to God? What do we receive from them that supports us in our life's journey? Consider a current movie, television series, or video game and what deep existential human desire it conveys. Does it delve into the problem of suffering, the need for forgiveness, the power of hope, or the purpose of our existence? Pondering these desires can lead us to turn to God for the answers to all the questions and yearnings of our soul. As the Psalmist says, "The Lord is near . . . to all who call on him in truth." God embraces us in our search for him.

The practice of *cinema divina* is a way to pray with the movies and television series we watch and the video games we play. It mirrors *lectio divina*, an ancient form of praying the Scriptures. *Cinema divina* uses Scripture that connects with a theme in the visual story. This practice can show us how, when seen through the lens of the word of God, the story reflects God's grace at work in human creativity.

Next time you watch a movie or television series, try praying with it through the process of *cinema divina* (see Appendix D). The *cinema divina* method of prayer allows you to enter more profoundly into the story, discovering its lessons and values pertinent to your life.

*God, Divine Storyteller, speak to me in and through the cinematic and visual stories with which I engage. Open my heart to hear your voice calling me to reflect deeply on my life and my relationship with you. Thank you for the story of my life!*

*Week 4 Wednesday*

# Celebrity Icons

But the Lord said to Samuel, "Do not look on his appearance or on the height of his stature, because I have rejected him; for the Lord does not see as mortals see; they look on the outward appearance, but the Lord looks on the heart."

*—1 Samuel 16:7*

As a film reviewer in Hollywood, I attend press junkets to interview directors, producers, and actors. I was once with other journalists interviewing the legendary actor Harrison Ford. Pleased to see a religious sister present, he gave me a big smile and greeting. Afterward, I went up to him, shook his hand, and said, "As Pauline Sisters, we pray for all those who work in media. So, you have a whole group of nuns praying for you in a special way." He looked at me with surprise, closed his eyes, and said, "Thank you so much. That means more to me than you know."

We might not consider the challenges celebrities face in their daily lives. Though they may have fame and fortune, they also face difficulties because of that status. And regardless of their fame, they are human beings like us with good and bad days, joys and sorrows, blessings and pains. We see the externals of their lives while God looks at the heart, as the Lord tells Samuel.

As we examine our own media use during our fast, we can pray for those people we hold as icons, as well as for those whose mistakes the public sees and hears about. Let us remember that the Lord knows their deepest desires and needs. Praying for those we admire also reminds us of their humanity, as well as their ability to influence society for good or ill. We pray especially that they may fulfill their God-given mission to use their powerful status for good, and that they may turn to God and be open to the truth.

Prayer for cultural influencers allows us to go deeper into the reality of the popular culture to recognize the yearnings of the human person, instead of seeing only the superficial image. As cultural mystics, we can recognize the human struggles of celebrities and transform the culture through our prayerful intercession for their needs and intentions.

Today, pray for a celebrity you admire. Use the method of the Novena of Prayer for Celebrities (see Appendix D). Offer that person up to the Lord with gratitude for his or her gifts and ask God to intercede for his or her needs and intentions.

*Jesus, you are my Life and the One in whom I find complete fulfillment. Inspire those who are famous cultural icons to seek you as their eternal good. May they use their influence to promote human dignity and give glory to you as their Savior.*

*WEEK 4 THURSDAY*

# Pop Culture Catechism

For by grace you have been saved through faith, and this is not your own doing; it is the gift of God—not the result of works, so that no one may boast. For we are what he has made us, created in Christ Jesus for good works, which God prepared beforehand to be our way of life.

*—Ephesians 2:8–10*

EPHESUS AT THE TIME of Paul was a significant seaport city in the ancient world, where Gentiles from every ethnicity commingled and traded their crafts as well as their religious practices. Their idols showed that they longed for a personal God. When Paul visited them preaching the saving message of Christ, they received it with joy. Their idols were inanimate objects, not a living person like Jesus Christ, both God and man. Paul engaged with the people within the popular cultural environment by addressing their deepest desires. He became the instrument of God's creative gift for the Ephesians who longed for the Good News.

We, too, can connect our faith with our pop culture experience and engage others in deeper reflection.

Online discussions connecting *Star Wars* and theology get accolades from fellow sci-fi enthusiasts. Once I posted on social media a comment about how the dark side of the Force represents the evil that entices us, while the light side of the Force inspires the choice for good. The struggle between them is reminiscent of the eternal struggle between angels and demons, between God and Satan, and the same struggle goes on within each of us. A young woman commented on how that inspired her, although she no longer had faith. I told her I'd pray for her. Months later, I saw a post from her blog. In the post, she reviewed a contemporary sci-fi show, making deep theological connections and even commenting that the presence of a religious sister among the show's characters reminded her that she had once considered a religious vocation. Her reflection on the show led her to consider faith in God once again.

By bringing our faith into dialogue with pop culture, we can guide others to deeper reflection. When we engage them on familiar ground, we can then propose Christ as the One who fulfills all their longings, as Saint Paul did with the Ephesians. They not only accepted Christ as Savior but also changed their lives by putting aside idols and magic. Their actions inspired the magicians and sorcerers to burn their books and turn to the Living God. When we discover ways that faith elements are present in cultural stories and draw out the deeper meanings for others, we offer a pop culture catechesis and so can influence our contemporary culture for good.

The next time you watch a movie, listen to an audiobook, or read a webcomic, make a comment or write a short review about how you see God in the story or the human needs it addresses. Invite others to respond to your reflection and create a dialogue about Christ in pop culture. Pray for those who are searching, that your engagement may lead them to faith in Christ.

*Master and Creator, through love you bring creativity into the world. You inspire storytellers to reflect on what it means to be human. Help me to reflect on these stories and communicate the faith connections, seeing them as opportunities for engagement with others who may be searching for you.*

# Saints as Cultural Mystics

Here is a call for the endurance of the saints, those who keep the commandments of God and hold fast to the faith of Jesus.

*—Revelation 14:12*

WE MAY KNOW SOME holy people who "keep the commandments of God and hold fast to the faith of Jesus." Perhaps we can think of living or deceased people we have known personally, or we can look to the examples of the saints. Some such people may inspire us because their interests, careers, or familial backgrounds are similar to our own. The saints are human beings like us who faced their challenges with radical trust in God. They communicated the Gospel through the media of their day; now they can help us to become more media mindful and to live as cultural mystics.

I have many favorite saints, but a few stand out for me above the rest. Carlo Acutis, a fifteen-year-old gamer, loved Christ present in the Eucharist. He went to daily Mass and Communion and created a website of all the recorded Eucharistic miracles. Born in England but raised in Italy, Carlo spent time with technology and saw its potential for good. He died in 2006 from leukemia but left behind an example of holiness, being the first millennial and first gamer to be recognized as a saint. He's the person we pray to in our house when the Wi-Fi goes down!

Blessed James Alberione, an Italian priest, saw the need for people to become familiar with the word of God and the truth of Jesus Christ. His goal was to have the Bible in every home and to use technological inventions for good. In the early twentieth century he founded a new religious family, the Paulines, made up of ten institutes whose mission in the Church is to take on the mind, attitudes, and heart of Christ and communicate Christ through all forms of media, after the example of the great apostle-evangelizer Saint Paul. Alberione personally oversaw the printing of the Bible in more than fifty languages and became the first biblical film-maker in Italy. He saw the potential of every form of media to proclaim all that is good, true, and beautiful. He is known as the "Media Apostle of the New Evangelization."

In the twelfth century, Saint Hildegard of Bingen saw how art, music, and poetry reveal truths about God and humanity. She created the first morality play, a drama that personifies moral qualities as main characters presenting lessons about good moral conduct. She also composed the music and lyrics of the larg-est surviving collection of chants from the Middle Ages. Even though she did not have the same technology available to her that we have today, Saint Hildegard is an example of someone who used the media of her times to inspire spiritual yearnings in her audience.

No matter in what era they lived, the saints held fast to the faith. They communicated Christ through their natural talents and the media of their time. Saint Paul the Apostle wrote let-ters to the faith communities he founded. Saint Catherine of Bologna painted miniature portraits and illuminated manu-scripts used by popes and kings. Saint Maximilian Kolbe broad-cast radio programs about the Blessed Virgin Mary at the time of Nazi Germany.

How can these holy people be guides for a digital culture? Aware of the power of the media for good or ill, they show us how to tell the Good News by using the gifts God gives us.

————————o◯o————————

Pray the Litany of Media Saints for Media Mindfulness (see Appendix C) sometime today, asking for the saints' intercession to be more media mindful and to become a cultural mystic. Perhaps you can learn about one of the saints in the litany, using your media to grow in faith during or after this fast.

*Lord of all creation, you call men and women of every time and place to be your special communicators of grace to the people of their era. Help me to center my life completely on you so that I may be a saint for our digital age.*

# Mary, the First Influencer

The angel said to [Mary], "The Holy Spirit will come upon you, and the power of the Most High will overshadow you; therefore the child to be born will be holy; he will be called Son of God. And now, your relative Elizabeth in her old age has also conceived a son; and this is the sixth month for her who was said to be barren. For nothing will be impossible with God." Then Mary said, "Here am I, the servant of the Lord; let it be with me according to your word." Then the angel departed from her.

*—Luke 1:35–38*

I GREW UP CONSCIOUS of the Blessed Mother's role in my life and her influence before her Son for all who call upon her. Her presence was visible through the various media of statues, images, books, and holy cards strewn about our house. As a teenager, through family rosary nights and novenas, I prayed to Mary, asking her to help me know what God wanted of me in life. When I first met the Daughters of St. Paul, the Sisters gave me a prayer card to Mary entitled "To Know One's Own Vocation." I brought it to Mass and prayed, "Help me know my vocation," then added, "as long as it's not a nun!" I suppose Mary had a good laugh when I entered the convent a year later! Her familiar presence had influenced my vocation to religious life.

No other person in history has wielded such a powerful influence before God as Mary, the Mother of Jesus. When the Angel Gabriel announced God's extraordinary plan to use her as the instrument to express God's superabundant love for humanity, heaven and earth waited for her response. Her "yes" to God's will influenced the trajectory of the whole world. She became the media, so to speak, through which God communicates salvation to all human beings of every time and place. Hers is not a static transmission, but rather an active participation in the creative development of God's saving message in Christ. Not only did she accept becoming the Mother of God, but she immediately went to communicate the message of salvation to her cousin Elizabeth. Her form of communication was the spoken word in her proclamation of the Magnificat, "My soul magnifies the Lord" (Lk 1:46). In the words of Pope Francis, she becomes "the most influential woman in history,"[34] God's first social influencer.

If you look up hashtags and user names on social media related to the Blessed Mother, you will find hundreds of thousands of memes, images, videos, and followers. Her influence reaches into the digital sphere. Through her positive response to God, Mary becomes a conduit of grace that influences humanity as we long for a Savior. She shows us how to be cultural mystics, disciples of Christ who engage the culture with the message of the Gospel by following God's will in our lives.

Today, share your favorite image of Mary or prayer to her on a social media platform. If your fast includes these media, then pray a Rosary for the intention of knowing and persevering in your vocation.

*Mary, Mother, Teacher, and Queen, lead me to recognize God's grace in my life and help me to respond to his invitations to follow him in the vocation he desires of me. Through my "yes" to God, may my life become a communication of God's love for humanity and influence the culture for good.*

# Media Fast Check-in

Digital fasting includes taking time for prayer. How did you pray for and with your media this week? What difference did it make in your relationship to your media?

## Prayer in Reparation for the Misuse of the Media

*My Lord, I see digital media's potential for good as well as for evil. Today I appeal to your Divine Mercy for all media creators who use this technology to spread disinformation and multiply cybercriminal activity. May my fasting sacrifice make reparation for the sins committed through the misuse of these gifts. Amen.*

## You Can Do This

To be ready to meet the Lord at the end of life is the goal of holiness. As Christians, we aspire to live forever with Jesus, but we also are called to lead others to heaven. We do so by being cultural mystics: pondering the existential questions of humanity found in the cultural stories and proposing Christ as the answer. By our evangelizing witness of faith, let us inspire others to think of heaven.

> We must always lead others towards heaven. But we must lead those who live today, not those who lived ten or more centuries ago. We have to take the world and humanity as they are today, in order to do good today.[35]

> —Blessed James Alberione

## Life Hack for the Week

Every time you're tempted to feel jealous of a media influencer or celebrity, say one Hail Mary for that person.

# WEEK 5

# Creating Communion

The soul that unites itself to God has but one aspiration: Love.[36]

*—Blessed James Alberione*

AFTER MANY YEARS OF being unable to attend any high school reunions because I was stationed far from my hometown, I was delighted when I was living in New York and a former high school friend tracked me down. Though I would not be able to attend that year's reunion, my friend said she wanted me to give an update about what I'd been up to for the last decade or so. So, I put together a visual and some details about my life for her to share. She called me after the reunion and said I was the highlight of the night! Everyone wanted to know how I managed to remain a nun. Soon after that, many classmates started friending me on Facebook and following me on Instagram. Because of those connections, I have even met up with several long-lost high school friends. After years of busy lives, careers, and families, we began to connect once again, finding joy in the shared memories and blessings in the new ones.

The great promise of social networks is to instantly connect people with one another across time and geographical spaces. These social platforms expand our visions beyond our immediate experiences and extend the reach of our interactions. We can seek out those who have similar tastes, interests, careers, or acquaintances, many of whom we do not know in person. Our digital relationships fulfill a basic need for connection. They don't completely fill that need, which is why we continue to long for deeper communion with others, but they do satisfy it to a certain extent, especially if we use our media well.

Yet our social media use can also contribute to a deep sense of loneliness or a worsening of mental health issues. It is important to seek professional help if we struggle with regulating our mental health. Using our media in more community-oriented ways, such as forming prayer groups online or a chat room around a shared interest, may be another way to combat those oppressive feelings of loneliness. Forming caring relationships and a supportive community sustains us on the journey of life.

God created human beings to be in relationship. We long for it. We seek it. Because God, who is a communion of love between the three Divine Persons, made us in his image and likeness, we are not meant to be alone. We are created to be in a dynamic relationship of love.

## Jesus the Perfect Communicator

The Trinity, three Divine Persons in one God, expresses that communion of love in relationship with one another. In this divine union of persons there is a continual communication of love. Communication is a process of sharing life and information. As human beings, we do that both verbally and nonverbally through symbols, signs, words, or gestures. So we communicate love by our attitudes, words, and actions. God communicates his love through the Holy Spirit in the person of Jesus Christ, both God and man. In Christ, God communicates his very self to humanity through Jesus' signs and miracles, the greatest of which is the Resurrection. By his humanity, Jesus draws us into relationship with the Father and the Spirit, bringing all of humanity into that connection with God. He has not only shown us that relationship by spending time alone in prayer; he also teaches us to be familiar with God in the greatest prayer, the Our Father. Through Christ we enter into the Trinitarian communion of love.

Jesus Christ, the eternal Word spoken by the Father, shares the love of God with humanity. In the Gospels, Jesus communicates God's desire to save humanity from its sins. He shows us how to communicate in a way that gives life to others. Jesus says, "If you abide in me, and my words abide in you, ask for whatever you wish, and it will be done for you. My Father is glorified by this, that you bear much fruit and become my disciples" (Jn 15:7–8).

Jesus shows us that the ultimate goal of communication is to offer self-giving love to each person, bringing all into communion with God and one another. He calls the disciples and teaches them about the kingdom of God through examples of love and forgiveness. He heals lepers and other people on the peripheries of society so they can experience wholeness. When he prepares to make his sacrificial offering of love through his passion, death, and resurrection, he instructs the disciples to love one another as he has loved them (see Jn 13:34). Everything Jesus says and does communicates God's unconditional love for humanity and his desire for us to love him and others in return.

## Creating Digital Communion

Communication in the Christian sense, then, involves sacrifice, selflessness, and genuine concern for others. We look to Jesus as the authentic self-communication of God in love with humanity. As Jesus reached out to heal those he encountered, he invites us to reach out to others. When we look beyond ourselves to others, we can bring them into the Trinitarian communion of Love.

Our media fast guides us to grow in communion with others and with God. Stepping back from our media can lead us to reflect on the needs of those we interact with online without the distractions of pop-up advertising or video reels, as well as the needs of those around us. When we are aware of people's needs, we can see others with the eyes of Christ, who looks at each person with love, communicates life, and generates communion. After our media fast, we can create digital communion by being instruments of unity in digital spaces, bringing people together to share faith and life.

WEEK 5 SUNDAY

# Echo Chamber Prejudices

There is no longer Jew or Greek, there is no longer slave or free, there is no longer male and female; for all of you are one in Christ Jesus.

—*Galatians 3:28*

A PRIEST TOLD ME about his thirty-year friendship with an atheist. They are polar opposites when it comes to politics and religion, but they enjoy one another's company and share about what they do have in common—love of art and movies. For these two unlikely friends, the media provide a point of unity, when so often our media are causes of contention and polarization.

Too often it's easy to dismiss others who think, look, or act differently than we do. Social media facilitate polarizing behavior. When we seek out and follow only those news sources and influential people who share our views, or when an algorithmic function creates a repetition of perspectives that reinforce our pre-existing beliefs and eliminates opposing views, we enter an "echo chamber." The echo-chamber mentality can prevent us from having nuanced conversations about challenging topics with people online or in-person because it steeps us in our own worldview's rhetoric. If these echo chambers cause us to deliberately block people online or cut off contact in-person because of an online argument or differences of views on a polarizing topic, then we can take time during this fast to assess our underlying prejudices.

How can we relate to people who are different from ourselves? How can we develop an integrative worldview open to various cultures, perspectives, and faith experiences? We can start by checking our media use for potential echo chambers and working to defeat our biases both in-person and online. It takes cultural humility: the practice of critical self-reflection on our own worldview as well as lifelong learning about other people's worldviews and cultural experiences.

Cultural humility also includes respecting the life and dignity of every human being, which is the first principle of Catholic social teaching.[37] We can use our media to affirm this truth by seeking out news stories that promote human dignity and by following reputable people on social media who have various backgrounds or worldviews. A Catholic understanding of diversity does not involve agreeing with or supporting those who directly advocate for anything that contradicts the Gospel; rather, it respects a variety of perspectives and cultural experiences while upholding the teachings of the Church. If instead we allow prejudices in our worldview to influence our media experience, we will end up in a polarized echo chamber, creating "us" and "them" scenarios. This goes against the Catholic social teaching principle of solidarity, which recognizes that we are all brothers and sisters in one human family regardless of national, religious, economic, ideological, or other differences.

Solidarity is about seeking justice and peace for all people. It means going beyond the media echo chambers to create genuine understanding. In the words of Saint Pope Paul VI: "If you want peace, work for justice."[38] He continues, "More greatness of soul is needed for yielding to the ways of Justice and Peace than for fighting for and imposing on an adversary one's rights, whether true or alleged."[39]

In our increasingly polarized world, peace and justice include respect for each person we encounter online and in-person. We can only change the world if we begin by changing ourselves. The more we change as Saint Paul exhorts, believing that we are all one in Christ, the more we treat each person as Christ himself.

———————————o○o———————————

What is your level of cultural humility? What prejudice lingers in your heart? Pray about this. Ask the Lord for forgiveness and the strength to be his instrument of solidarity in the world.

*Jesus, you call me to love others as you love me. Each person is my brother or sister, who begs for my care, concern, and respect. Change my prejudices into charity, my animosity into love.*

*WEEK 5 MONDAY*

# Gaming Groups

Two are better than one, because they have a good reward for their toil. For if they fall, one will lift up the other; but woe to one who is alone and falls and does not have another to help.

—*Ecclesiastes 4:9–10*

HUMAN BEINGS FORM COMMUNITIES around shared interests, beliefs, and values. In a digital culture, video games spawn the largest online communities. The gaming industry boasts more profit than movies and sports combined, with revenues well over $200 billion worldwide and an annual increase of 13 percent.[40]

I once gave a presentation to theologians about the ethics of massively multiplayer online role-playing games (MMORPGs). I spoke about real communities formed around shared gaming interests. One woman came up to me afterward to thank me for not bashing video games. She had expected that I would respond negatively to online relationships surrounding video games, since other theologians only brought out the negative consequences of gaming. She shared that she is a gamer and sees the value of online communities.

It's true that excessive use of video games can create a sense of isolation or desensitize us to violence; however, many games, like *Minecraft* or *Call of Duty*, encourage players to develop skills as members of a team. Multiplayer games create communities. Together, gaming groups explore the field of different games' creative landscapes and tactics with real-time communication. Gamer-sharing platforms like Twitch, Reddit, and Discord allow gamers to connect with others while posting strategies and comments on new game features.

Gaming groups can also help players navigate real-life problems outside of the gaming world. A MMORPG gaming group once noticed that a member was not responding well to the chat, so they tried to help him communicate about what he was going through. They guided him through a depression episode rife with suicidal thoughts. By being present to him in his struggles through listening and understanding, the gaming group saved his life. They were a true community where the gamer found the help he needed.

Like the story above, the author of Ecclesiastes offers some insight into our innate human need for community. It is always better, he says, to form relationships, since without others in our lives we have no one to pick us up when we fall. God is always there for us, but we also need other people—both online and face-to-face—for support. We are social beings who grow from our interactions with others. If they truly care about us, other people want us to become the best we can be. They desire our good, as our Heavenly Father desires goodness and love for each of us.

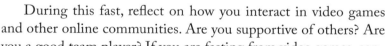

During this fast, reflect on how you interact in video games and other online communities. Are you supportive of others? Are you a good team player? If you are fasting from video games, consider the balance between your online community and your face-to-face relationships, and the time you give to both. Do you treat people the same online as in person?

*Heavenly Father, you want me to live as my best self and to grow in my relationships with others. Help me to be a good team player, supporting those who need a listening ear or an understanding heart.*

*Week 5 Tuesday*

# Concert Connection

Let us hold fast to the confession of our hope without wavering, for he who has promised is faithful. And let us consider how to provoke one another to love and good deeds, not neglecting to meet together, as is the habit of some, but encouraging one another, and all the more as you see the Day approaching.

—*Hebrews 10:23–25*

Taylor Swift's concerts defy generational gaps, bringing together tween girls, middle-aged dads, and everyone in between, offering a sense of solidarity and ritual. Not only do Swifties create and share friendship bracelets with other concert-goers, but they also commune together over Taylor's inside jokes and Easter eggs, which she drops before, during, and after her concert tours.

Some fans compare Taylor's concerts to going to church, saying, "It was the most religious experience of my life!" In stadiums filled with tens of thousands of people, fans experience something bigger than themselves. Her music, many feel, is a celebration that takes them out of their everyday drudgery into an emotional high. Their experience of the common rituals and intermixing old and new songs and traditions addresses the need for belonging and connection across generations. The way Swift expresses her struggles with darkness and pain to her audience with authenticity and freedom speaks to the depths of their souls and their yearning for something greater than what this world offers.

In a digitally isolated world, we long for a sense of belonging and a shared passion that uplifts even when life's challenges overwhelm us. We long for something to believe in that is beyond ourselves. Music heals and speaks to spiritual desires for something more, something beyond a concert high, that connects us with one another.

A concert may provide feelings of elation, encouragement, and belonging, but these feelings eventually fade, leaving us disenchanted the next time we face life's hurdles. Instead, Christ offers a hope that does not disappoint (see Rom 5:5). In him, the one who sacrificed his life for us, we find our sense of belonging through a worshipping community of faith. The communion of saints, the great "cloud of witnesses" (Heb 12:1), helps us believe in something beyond ourselves—in the God through whom music, art, and beauty itself exist. The Letter to the Hebrews tells us to hold fast to the "confession of our hope without wavering, for he who promised is faithful." The Eucharistic liturgy is a communal celebration of God's faithfulness to us in Christ. It offers a lasting joy that is deeper than a concert high. Christ alone can fulfill the deepest desires of our hearts and heal our wounds through the sacramental rituals of Reconciliation and Eucharist. These sacred rituals equip us not only with a feeling of joy but with grace, Christ's actual presence in our souls.

Whether you have found a sense of community at a concert or in another media experience, bring that need for authentic communion to your everyday life by joining or creating a prayer group, inviting people to a praise and worship Holy Hour, attending Mass with others, or ritualizing a regular prayer time with friends. Afterward, gather at a pub or café and share about faith and life.

*Jesus, you know my desire for meaningful connection and community. I want the companionship of other people with whom I can share authentic spiritual desires and experiences of faith and hope. Lead me to celebrate your life with others like me who are seeking spiritual connection and communion.*

# Recognizing Our Humanity

"For if you love those who love you, what reward do you have? Do not even the tax collectors do the same? And if you greet only your brothers and sisters, what more are you doing than others? Do not even the Gentiles do the same? Be perfect, therefore, as your heavenly Father is perfect."

*—Matthew 5:46–48*

MOST GAME APP CREATORS recognize our loyalty by offering incentives that keep us interested in the game. Online shopping sites suggest additional items based on our purchases. And social media algorithms present posts from accounts we interact with the most. Such incentives show that they are attentive to our presence. But the type of attention that keeps us gaming, shopping, or viewing is not enough to fulfill our need for recognition.

We all want to be recognized and appreciated for who we are. We long for the warmth and complexity of human relationships. Both our digital and in-person relationships need our recognition and engagement to endure. Acknowledging someone's humanity requires going beyond doing the bare minimum. Texting an encouraging emoji, giving money to a homeless person, or holding the door for someone are courteous actions. But to be perfect, as today's Scripture calls us to be, means to encounter and interact with people on a deeper level.

A CBS news station in Florida ran a story on a local barber who took his grooming supplies and hit the streets, offering the homeless free haircuts and backpacks filled with hygiene supplies. He makes a connection with them by talking and sharing stories.

They trust him to give them a fresh start through a haircut. Having experienced addiction and homelessness in his past, Greg Young knows the importance of relying on God and acknowledging the humanity of another. He's on a mission to bring hope and dignity to those most in need. After the news story aired, he received offers to donate to his cause and so started the Backpack Barber Foundation. Through social media, he raises awareness of the stories of the people he encounters on the streets and uses the donations he receives to make a difference in their lives. Young offers a video message online to anyone who may be experiencing a difficult time, saying, "If nobody today tells you they love you, Greg the barber loves you, baby!" and "Peace, stay blessed, y'all."[41]

Jesus calls us to go the extra mile like Greg Young and *be love* in the world. We can donate a dollar to someone who is in need, but more importantly, we can encounter and interact with him or her as a beautiful human being created by God. Jesus' words challenge us to bring love where there is no love. Daily life provides multiple opportunities online and in-person to recognize and appreciate others, especially those who are most hidden or overlooked by society. How can we be perfect like our Heavenly Father? It begins with the Gospel maxim, "love one another."

What persons in your life, online or in-person, need your engagement? How can you encounter them on a deeper level, so they know they are loved and appreciated? Fortify that relationship by reaching out to them today.

*Lover of all, may my life be a communication of your love to others. Help me see that everyone desires to be loved and appreciated. Make me aware of the persons I meet and challenge me to go beyond the bare minimum to love as you love them.*

*WEEK 5 THURSDAY*
# Gauging Authentic Friendships

Some friends play at friendship
but a true friend sticks closer than one's nearest kin.
—*Proverbs 18:24*

PROBABLY NOTHING IN POP culture expresses authentic friendship as well as Sam and Frodo's relationship in *The Lord of the Rings*. They share life, pain, sorrow, and joy as they support each other on their impossible mission to Mordor. Going into the fire together, they come out even more united in an unbreakable bond of friendship. Friendship is the core of social media, though we also use social media for professional networking, business, and sharing faith. Our online relationships may be a little less dramatic than Sam and Frodo's, but they can be meaningful and authentic if they, like face-to-face interactions, are genuine, mutual, and life-giving.

This fast gives us the opportunity to evaluate our online friendships to determine if they are dependable and support our becoming the best version of ourselves. The way to gauge relationships is the same online as in person. Authentic friends should lead each other closer to God and help each other grow in virtue. Three particular qualities to look for are mutuality, genuineness, and peace.

Saint Aelred of Rievaulx writes about the value of friendship in his classic work *Spiritual Friendship*. He says, "No remedy is more powerful, effective, and distinctive in everything that fills this life than to have someone to share your every loss with compassion and your every gain with congratulations."[42] The deepest value of friendship lies in being present to and for one another. When people look for deep friendships, online or in person, the first good quality in a relationship should be mutuality, as in the case of Sam and Frodo taking turns helping one another. Is there a balanced give and take, or does the giving seem one-sided?

Another gauge in relationships is genuineness. Can each person be his or her genuine self with the other and feel accepted? There will still be differences of opinion, but these differences can be opportunities for us to grow in learning how to communicate well during crucial conversations. In a genuine friendship, despite these differences, each person is clearly appreciated and loved. Genuine friendship and love hinge on seeking the good of the other—always. Sam seeks the good for his friend when he emboldens Frodo's dampened spirits and encourages him to persevere by saying, "There's some good in this world, Mr. Frodo. And it's worth fighting for."[43]

Peace is a result of mutual respect in relationships coming from trust. This is true for any relationship where we make ourselves vulnerable to another person, as Frodo trusts Sam to take care of him in perilous situations and Sam trusts Frodo to complete their mission. We trust that our friend has our best interest at heart and vice versa. Reciprocal trust creates peace in a relationship, which is a sign we are following God's will for our lives.

Use your extra time during this fast to consider whether mutuality, genuineness, and peace are present in your relationships. Take a moment today to check the authenticity of your online and in-person friendships.

*Jesus, my true Friend, in a digital world, genuine friendships are sometimes hard to come by. Help me to wait with patience and work on growing in virtue so I can form good friendships and be an authentic friend to those friends I have already. Help me realize that true love and friendship bring me closer to you and make me the best version of myself, providing joy and undisputed happiness.*

*WEEK 5 FRIDAY*

# FOMO

I know what it is to have little, and I know what it is to have plenty. In any and all circumstances I have learned the secret of being well-fed and of going hungry, of having plenty and of being in need. I can do all things through him who strengthens me.

—*Philippians 4:12–13*

IN A CONSTANT STREAM of information on multiple social media platforms, we receive up-to-date news about everything everyone is doing at all times. It's amazing—but exhausting! We receive notifications of a friend's new video post, an acquaintance's work anniversary on their LinkedIn profile, another friend's fabulous vacation pictures on Instagram, and a new viral TikTok trend. We might worry about missing something when we don't check our social media. An inevitable feeling takes us over—FOMO.

FOMO (fear of missing out) refers to the perception that others are having more fun, more opportunities, or more experiences than we are. This perception of missing out on social connection is often caused by these digital sharing platforms and can lead to a compulsive need to maintain all of our connections. It can create a sense of envy and low self-esteem. It ultimately derives from unhappiness that we are not like those social influencers we admire or from the fear of not being as liked or connected as others. These feelings are greater in people who experience low levels of life satisfaction. The anxiety created from the fear of missing out comes from an unhealthy, self-centered preoccupation about our place in a community and can lead us to create false divisions while withdrawing from other people.

I once asked a group of teenagers what social media platforms they engage in. Snapchat? Hands raised. YouTube? Hands up. Instagram? Very few hands went up. I asked, "Why not Instagram?" One young woman responded, "It leads to all kinds of comparisons, jealousies, and divisions." She had decided she wanted none of that in her relationships nor the anxiety that came with it. Her insight described the effects of FOMO.

As we are learning through this fast, we don't necessarily need to remove media from our lives, but using media wisely does require thoughtful choices. I commended the young woman for discerning how to choose relationships over unhealthy comparisons, regardless of what she might miss out on as a result. Being mindful of our media means making choices for the good of our whole selves—mind, body, and spirit.

In his letter to the Philippians, Saint Paul says that he finds satisfaction in his external life circumstances regardless of what they are, since what matters is his relationship with Christ. In Christ, he says, "I can do all things through him who strengthens me." It doesn't matter whether we are the most "in the know" or the most popular, or whether we have the perfect-seeming lifestyle of the people we follow. What matters is that we do not "miss out" on our relationship with Jesus Christ!

Christ leads us to communion with others. In Christ, FOMO disappears. Feelings of self-worth connected to how (or how much) others think of us can be transformed when we put Christ first in our hearts. Christ inspires us to engage in a community in a healthier way where we share life and faith.

Whether or not you are fasting from social media, consider these questions when you return to scrolling your feed: When I see someone else's positive posts, do I turn in on myself, feel jealous, or withdraw into my feelings of dissatisfaction? If those negative feelings arise, do I turn to Christ in prayer and/or reach out to connect with someone?

*Heavenly Father, so many times I feel left out after seeing the lifestyles of others on social media. Calm my anxiety and help me to recognize that my relationships with you and with other people around me are more important than social media influence or apparent perfection. Thank you for the many gifts you have given me that only I can share with the world.*

WEEK 5 SATURDAY

# Digital Prayer

Likewise the Spirit helps us in our weakness; for we do not know how to pray as we ought, but that very Spirit intercedes with sighs too deep for words. And God, who searches the heart, knows what is the mind of the Spirit, because the Spirit intercedes for the saints according to the will of God.

*—Romans 8:26–27*

SOMETIMES WE MAY HAVE time for silent prayer but feel we don't know what to say to God. Maybe we wonder if there are ways to incorporate prayer into our digital experience once this fast ends. Or we may ponder how we can create or connect to a community of believers online to keep our prayer life alive. As we conclude this week of reflecting on communion, we can consider that prayer, more than anything else, is about communing with God, our Creator and Redeemer.

Christian prayer is personal but also communal. When we pray as Christians, we join with Christ, who prayed to the Father for the coming of God's kingdom. And our prayer involves the whole community of believers. The Mass or Eucharistic Liturgy is the best form of prayer because we unite ourselves with Christ's sacrifice on the altar together with the community. But we can even be part of the Church's prayer online. Catholic prayer apps teach Catholic meditation and prayer in simple and creative ways. Through these apps, we can join with thousands of other people praying the same novena or Marian consecration.

Online prayer apps or groups help people to connect with God and with each other. For example, one woman started a private group chat to share saint quotes during Lent. The group expanded as members added friends and acquaintances who were interested. People shared prayer intentions, and the chat became a place for members to pray for one another, even if they didn't know each other in real life. The communal dimension of prayer includes intercessory prayer for the needs of others and creates communion among believers.

Either now or when the fast is over, depending on what type of media fast you are doing, consider using a Catholic prayer app to support your relationship with God. Or, if so inspired, you can create or join an online prayer community for particular needs or intentions.

*Holy Spirit, sometimes I can't find the proper words to express my thoughts and feelings in prayer. Give me the words, even through prayer apps, so that I may enter into communion with you and unite my prayer with others online.*

# Media Fast Check-in

As you review this week of your fast, what did you learn about your relationships with those closest to you? How has less screen time changed the way you relate to them?

## Prayer in Reparation for the Misuse of the Media

*Heavenly Father, I call down your mercy on all who are led away from your fatherly love by the misuse of the media. I offer to you all my sacrifices during this fast so that my efforts may contribute to building a world of peace and unity. God of salvation, love, and hope, enfold in your most tender embrace everyone who is searching for you. Amen.*

## You Can Do This

Every time we fall, we can pick ourselves up again. The same is true in the spiritual life. We may have lost our way during our fast, but we can always begin again.

> Don't lose heart. Always preserve a healthy optimism. History is the teacher of life, and our past experiences school us for the future. A battle lost, we have time as long as we live to succeed in another.[44]

—Blessed James Alberione

## Life Hack for the Week

In your calendar, reserve a fifteen-minute time slot each day for silent prayer. Set a notification as a reminder.

# WEEK 6

# Transforming the Culture

You don't have to go about worriedly trying to get rid of the darkness. Just turn on some light.[45]

—*Blessed James Alberione*

WE'VE COME THIS FAR in our fast, so we can begin to harvest the fruits of our efforts to grow in our relationships with God, others, and our media. During this fast we've allowed transformation to take place in us. The more we let God work in and through us, the more we can shine a light by transforming and influencing the culture for good.

Blessed Carlo Acutis, for example, went to daily Mass and Communion, though his parents were not practicing their faith. He was so faith-filled and inquisitive that the questions he asked his mother about God led her back to her Catholic roots. Imbued with Christ's presence in the consecrated bread and wine, Carlo wanted the world to be transformed, freed, and purified by this sacred presence. He said, "Since the Eucharist exists substantially and vitally, we must spread it through this current. It is a current which is called multimedia."[46] Carlo used his love of technology to create a website, still operating today, of all the recorded Eucharistic miracles throughout the ages. On another website he also started documenting all the Marian apparitions from around the world. When he was diagnosed with leukemia, he offered his life for the Church. His years-long devotion to Christ in the Eucharist had transformed him so that his suffering became an offering of love. He died in his teens in 2006, leaving behind an example of holiness—someone "eucharisticized,"[47] as he would say, totally incorporated into Christ. As the first millennial saint and first gamer saint, Carlo transformed the digital culture by influencing it for good.

## Spiritual Transformation

Like Blessed Carlo, we can observe how our media choices can lead to our own spiritual growth. The more we learn to let go of our desire for control, believing that God's love is infinite and that he desires what is best for us, the more we create a contagious aura of trust in God. The process of moving from control to surrender, despair to hope, anxiety to trust is called *spiritual transformation*. It is a movement of the spiritual life, through prayer and practice, to gradual *configuration* with Christ, that is, "putting on Christ." As we take on the mind and heart of Christ, we come to the point Saint Paul describes, where "It is no longer I who live, but it is Christ who lives in me" (Gal 2:20). When people see us, they see Christ.

The progress we've made in this media fast has transformed not only our relationship with God but also our relationship with our media. We have learned to use media in a holier and healthier way. Living in this manner, we can transform the culture for good while participating in our own spiritual transformation.

Authentic spiritual transformation in Christ involves confronting our patterns of sin, addictions, desire for control, and preoccupation with self so to make Christ the center of our lives. It's about putting our ego second to allow Christ to be visible in and through us. When we work on our spiritual lives in this way, we become a transforming force in all the places in which we interact and relate with others, including digital spaces. Occupying these spaces, we effect a cultural change from the inside out, transforming norms, shaping values for the good of the human family, and allowing Christ to be visible in all that is authentically human.

## Being a Transforming Presence

Sometimes what the culture proclaims as a source of happiness may simply be self-indulgence. Not that seeking to get a good job, advancing our financial prospects, buying a house, or taking a vacation are bad things! But we have to be careful not to lose sight of our spiritual lives while working for our material needs. In striving to obtain these goods, we may find ourselves in situations that challenge our moral core. Growth in our spiritual lives may embolden us to stand up for our faith, even in ethically challenging situations, in-person and online.

Our religious values are our guide when we are faced with ethical questions. If we encounter cheating, backbiting, stealing, or other sinful behaviors, we can act according to our faith instead of these problematic attitudes. Our moral actions can be a testimony to our faith and as such can place virtue at the center of the collective consciousness, changing others' hearts as well.

Our fast provides the space for us to consider how we live in the media culture. It especially gets us to reflect on if and how our relationship with Christ shows in the way we live our lives in-person and online. The more we attend to our spiritual life, the more we effect a change in our relationship to media so as to integrate our faith values into our daily media choices.

Amazing heroes like Carlo Acutis encourage us to never give up hope, and to always seek to witness to the transforming power of Christ's presence in our lives. As media creators, each of us shapes the culture by what we choose to communicate. As media consumers, we are shaped to some degree by what we choose to consume. In turn, this shapes the way we share our values and interact with those around us. May our lives be as impactful as were the lives of the saints!

*WEEK 6 SUNDAY*

# The Common Good

"This is my commandment, that you love one another as I have loved you. No one has greater love than this, to lay down one's life for one's friends. You are my friends if you do what I command you. I do not call you servants any longer, because the servant does not know what the master is doing; but I have called you friends, because I have made known to you everything that I have heard from my Father."

—*John 15:12–15*

LIFE HOLDS ADVENTURE AND promise. The best speeches convey that success in life is not measured by dollars but by strength of character and commitment to the common good. Booker T. Washington once said, "the best way to lift one's self up is to help some one else."[48] As Christians, Jesus challenges us to go one step further when he says, "love one another as I have loved you," which means to love unconditionally. Loving our enemies, forgiving those who slander our name online, offering a kind response to an obnoxious social media user, is loving as Jesus loves us. We betray him when we sin, but he still loves us so much that he offers his life for us on the cross. Love builds, supports, and nourishes communion. And that communion transforms a hurting society.

Teen siblings Hannah and Charlie Lucas created the notOK® app,[49] a virtual panic button, to help people struggling with mental illness to realize they are not alone and can reach out for help when needed. Diagnosed with POTS (Postural Orthostatic Tachycardia Syndrome) at fifteen, Hannah feared being alone, since she often fainted because of her condition. Her fears spiraled into severe depression and anxiety. At her lowest moment, contemplating self-harm, she instead developed the idea of the notOK® app to alert trusted contacts immediately that she needed help. Charlie was concerned about his older sister, and together they created their pre-crisis tool as a website, app, logo, and Bug and Bee, LLC company. His technical skills with her practical experience helped to develop a life-saving peer-support program for those struggling with mental health and other unexpected dangerous situations. It has been downloaded over 87,000 times, saving many lives.

How do we use our gifts for the common good in and through digital media? When we live each day with an others-centered focus and see each person as the image of Christ, we find creative ways to uplift others and bring them into community, as Hannah and Charlie did. A social media influencer raises awareness about human trafficking. A teacher creates an online campaign to collect school supplies for Catholic schoolchildren in underserved communities. A designer develops a series of Instagram stories to promote Eucharistic Adoration in the parish. A college student collects signatures through an online petition to advocate for accessibility for a physically challenged classmate. These simple gestures are ways we can use our media to contribute to the common good of society. Our upright character and attentiveness to the needs of others can change the world.

Today, consider supporting and raising awareness of a social cause through what you choose to share online. You may even create your own online advocacy for a social need and connect it to the outreach of a Catholic non-profit organization.

*Good and gracious God, you have given me some talents that I'd like to use for the good of others. You may not ask me to lay down my life for another, but I can give of myself by using my media for the good of others. Your friendship is all I desire in return.*

# Sacramental Worldview

And the Word became flesh and lived among us, and we have seen his glory, the glory as of a father's only son, full of grace and truth.

*—John 1:14*

STORYTELLERS USE SYMBOLISM IN visual and print media to communicate meaning. Eleven, the sacrificial character with supernatural powers in *Stranger Things*, must descend into the water to enter the parallel world of The Upside Down. Once submerged, she encounters the Demogorgon, or evil one, and seeks to protect others from his power. We can see Eleven's descent into the water as a symbol of Baptism, through which sin and death are overcome through the power of Christ. *Symbols* are material objects that point to abstract concepts. Material objects are also used by God to communicate his life and presence to us. We can recognize this if we develop a sacramental worldview.

Having a sacramental worldview means seeing God at work in and through the physical world and ordinary experiences of life. In a concrete, physical way, these perceptible elements and gestures indicate God's presence. This has been most tangible in the Incarnation. God became one with us by taking on human flesh in Christ. Jesus Christ is the sacrament of God's love for the world, the visible image of the invisible God (see Col 1:15). The mystery of the Incarnation, God mediated through human flesh, allows for a sacramental worldview where the material elements of the natural world signify the presence of God. A sacramental worldview is also rooted in the sacraments of the Church, which are visible signs of an invisible reality. God becomes present through perceptible elements. The result is a real change in our souls. The material elements reveal God's presence and action to us. For example, through the pouring of water with the words "I baptize you in the name of the Father, and of the Son, and of the Holy Spirit" in the sacrament of Baptism, the Trinity comes to live in the soul of the person being baptized.

If we look at symbols in media through a sacramental lens, we can see how water, for example, symbolizes cleansing from sin and restoration to new life in Christ. Water purifies, renews, and refreshes. In the classic Hayao Miyazaki anime film *Spirited Away*, the young girl Chihiro moves away from her neighborhood and becomes trapped in the realm of spirits. While in the spirit world, she works at a bathhouse that depends on river water to operate. She rescues a polluted river spirit by pouring excessive amounts of water on him, cleansing him from the all the garbage he's collected. She almost drowns, but the river spirit protects her, eventually leading to her liberation from the bathhouse witch.

With a sacramental worldview we discover that God is at work in everything, even in and through our technology and media stories. We can recognize God at work when we see a video on social media or receive a text from a friend that gives us the answer to something we have been praying about. Watching a noble character in a movie or video game display an act of mercy may be how God inspires us to do the same. The more we try to understand our common human experience through the symbols found in visuals, sounds, or music lyrics, the more we see God's grace in our everyday lives.

Contemplate the last storytelling media you saw or heard through the symbols used in the story. What do they represent? How does that enhance your understanding of the story and how God is speaking to you through it?

*Jesus, Sacrament of the Father, help me to see the world through the lens of your grace. You reveal yourself through the tangible world and in all that is genuinely human. May I be an instrument of your grace by being a sacramental presence to others.*

*WEEK 6 TUESDAY*

# Consumerism

And [Jesus] said to them, "Take care! Be on your guard against all kinds of greed; for one's life does not consist in the abundance of possessions."

*—Luke 12:15*

THE NEED TO CONSUME products and services shapes our culture's language, values, and societal norms. The media contribute to a consumerist mindset through algorithms tied to our spending habits to deliver us sponsored ads on websites and in our email inboxes. The ads demand immediacy and are mainly focused on responsibility to oneself,[50] feeding a deep-rooted individualism. We can become absorbed by the cycle of consumerism, contributing to a "desire-based economy."[51] For example, following technology trends can lead us to ditch our old devices into the nebulous tech landfill, adding to environmental waste. But becoming caught up in consumerism also leads to a dissatisfaction with ourselves. The cultural expectations to possess can leave us feeling empty.

Not only that, but when we are focused on obtaining material goods for ourselves, our awareness of an ethical responsibility for "the other" fades before an obsession with newness and immediacy. A consumer-culture worldview can distract us from concern for the needs of others in the global community or our responsibility for God's creation. As disciples of Jesus striving to live the Gospel message, we are called to radical social responsibility, which is the heart of the Catholic Church's social teaching. That means supporting human dignity and rights; the needs of the poor, vulnerable, family, and community; and rights of workers. It also means caring for the earth. This may be countercultural in a consumeristic society centered on the individual. Social responsibility is a Christian duty of justice that demands consideration of the other person—even when that means doing without the latest trend, or avoiding products that are not ethically sourced or that damage the environment.

Jesus warns his disciples against centering their lives around material things. He teaches that those who store up material treasures will eventually realize that they can't take anything into eternity. Instead, when we support other people, we experience a selflessness that brings inner joy, far from the momentary pleasure of possessing goods.

In the light of the larger social issues of hunger, homelessness, or ecological destruction, the latest consumer trends seem unimportant. Jesus challenges our first-world culture of wasteful consumerism and greed with a call to socially responsible action. Some ways we can embody the Gospel message include creating a social media group where people can sell or give away second-hand items, shopping at a thrift store instead of reinforcing "fast fashion," or donating used items to a Catholic charity that helps people struggling with poverty.

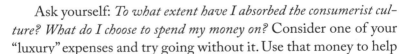

Ask yourself: *To what extent have I absorbed the consumerist culture? What do I choose to spend my money on?* Consider one of your "luxury" expenses and try going without it. Use that money to help someone in need or donate it to a charity.

*Jesus, you challenge me to check the material goods in my life while examining my attachment to them. Help me to detach myself from a consumerist way of life and to recognize the Church's call to social responsibility by reaching out to people in need.*

*WEEK 6 WEDNESDAY*

# Cancel Culture

We must no longer be children, tossed to and fro and blown about by every wind of doctrine, by people's trickery, by their craftiness in deceitful scheming. But speaking the truth in love, we must grow up in every way into him who is the head, into Christ, from whom the whole body, joined and knit together by every ligament with which it is equipped, as each part is working properly, promotes the body's growth in building itself up in love.

*—Ephesians 4:14–16*

CANCEL CULTURE IS A complex and controversial phenomenon that has taken root in our society and infiltrated many areas of our digital conversations. It is the public shaming or boycotting of individuals, organizations, or companies whose behavior or views are deemed offensive, whether they are actually problematic or simply at odds with mainstream cultural values. Cancel culture also involves condemning people or organizations because of past or present speech or behavior, with the intention of harming their reputation. They are often denied a public platform, reflecting the societal tension between accountability and the censoring of free speech.

Our culture suffers when we don't allow nuanced conversations to take place before digitally blocking someone with whom we disagree. One political commentator and comedian criticizes cancel culture as a form of "social murder" in which people are destroyed because of one social misstep. It has become harmful, this commentator declares, to open discourse as a means to arrive at truth. Authentic truth builds. It never destroys.

As Christians, we are called by Christ to "speak the truth in love," even when it's unpopular. And that may mean calling out the problems with "cancelling" other people, especially when that involves purposeful destruction of reputations or careers. It also entails willingness to speak charitably about unpopular truths, even at the risk of being "cancelled" ourselves. As disciples of Christ, we can transform the culture by how we engage in conversations around polarizing subjects. Our witness can prove that thoughtful dialogue is possible. Discerning how to engage in such conversations requires the skills of media mindfulness to determine what is acceptable, as in subtle commentary like satire, and which actions and opinions are actually harmful, such as explicit hate speech. Respect for the human person drives our critical engagement.

The Gospel continually reminds us that though we are sinners, Jesus gave of himself to redeem each of us. The Christian response to those who have fallen out of favor in the public eye is to recognize that everyone deserves a second chance to restore their reputation. Jesus gave that chance to the tax collector Matthew, the adulterous woman about to be stoned, and Peter after he denied Jesus three times. By labeling people according to their past wrongs or opinions, cancel culture denies that redemption is possible. Jesus, instead, calls people to conversion.

Today, instead of simply blocking people who hold problematic opinions, pray that they will change for the better. Pray also for a cultural change that will allow differing opinions to be held in balance with respect for the dignity of each human being.

*Jesus, our media culture suffers when people are condemned for their opinions and actions with no opportunity for redemption. Grant me the grace to examine social discourse with respect for each person and the courage to speak the truth with charity.*

*WEEK 6 THURSDAY*

# Culture of Life

For it was you who formed my inward parts;
　you knit me together in my mother's womb.
I praise you, for I am fearfully and wonderfully made.
　Wonderful are your works.

*—Psalm 139:13–14*

I CAME ACROSS THE most delightful viral video of an ultrasound screen during a pregnancy check up. As the couple sang and clapped their hands, the baby clapped along with the song! The parents laughed with such surprise that they kept singing and the baby continued to clap along. This simple video infuses a culture of life into a world of abortion debates.

Abortion is one of the most contested political and moral issues of our times. Most news outlets avoid reporting on pro-life events except from a negative viewpoint. Mainstream news rarely reports on the several hundred thousand pro-lifers peacefully marching in the annual March for Life in Washington, DC, but instead focuses on the smaller crowd of pro-abortion protesters, usually portraying them and their emphasis on choice as the more reasonable side. Other news stories downplay violent attacks on pregnancy centers or ignore them altogether; yet they will show the arrest of a pro-life person praying outside an abortion clinic. YouTube undermines videos with pro-life content by adding disclaimers and links below the videos, in which abortion is described using pro-choice terminology.

Recognizing these biases, we can reflect on how the media we consume do or don't present a culture of life. We can also consider whether we use media in a way that reflects the value of all human life. Do we respect each person we encounter online, or do we treat some people as inconvenient or as objects to be used? Do we consume media that depict the human person as expendable? Our personal choices can add to or detract from a culture of life.

We can also transform the culture by being informed about relevant pro-life issues and educating the public on the value of life through the media we create. One young Black pro-life woman from South Carolina found her path and followers on Tik-Tok when she questioned whether abortion clinics target African Americans, considering the high rate of Black women seeking abortions. Other pro-life groups garner followers by offering logical arguments for why abortion isn't the solution to various social problems.

Being pro-life also means having a consistent ethic related to all basic human rights. It involves standing for human dignity through all the stages and circumstances of life. If we believe in the value of each person, then abortion, euthanasia, assisted suicide, capital punishment, human trafficking, racism, poverty, and homelessness are all pro-life issues deserving of our attention and social action. In the same way, we create harmony between living a culture of life both in-person and online when we "speak the truth in love" (Eph 4:15), whether we engage the person face-to-face or anonymously through a screen. Our support of social causes both in-person and online that promote the dignity of every human being flows from a consistent ethic of life and creates a culture of life.

In your digital spaces, be a witness to a culture of life by what you post and share and which accounts you follow. Consider how to support others through one of the many Catholic pro-life or social justice organizations. Transform the culture by upholding the God-given gift of life, from conception to natural death, through the selfless love you show for others.

*Lord of all, you formed me in my mother's womb and gave me the breath of life. Give me the grace to support all human life, especially the most vulnerable. By helping me give of myself in love to others, may you work through me to bring about a cultural transformation from death to life.*

# A Communicative Love

> While they were eating, Jesus took a loaf of bread, and after blessing it he broke it, gave it to the disciples, and said, "Take, eat; this is my body." Then he took a cup, and after giving thanks he gave it to them, saying, "Drink from it, all of you; for this is my blood of the covenant, which is poured out for many for the forgiveness of sins."
>
> —Matthew 26:26–28

COMMUNICATION IS THE ACT of sharing or exchanging information. But it is also the act of giving of oneself by imparting ideas, thoughts, feelings, expressions, and love. A *communicative love*, one that stands always ready to share life, fosters intimate relationships.

Jesus communicates his love to us by giving of himself through his life, death, and resurrection, and in a lasting way through the Eucharist. In this sacrificial offering, Christ allows himself to be our food, in mass production and mass distribution. The Eucharist, in a sense, is the most powerful form of "media" or means of mass communication, as it communicates not only information but life itself!

Sister Clare Crockett's life became a communication of love between her soul and Christ present in the Eucharist. Born in 1982 in Derry, Northern Ireland, Clare became a flamboyant film and television actress and talented musician. She enjoyed the attention of the cameras, which were attracted to her magnetic personality. But her wild, superficial lifestyle of partying and drinking left her empty. She found herself on a retreat in Spain with the Sister Servants of the Home of the Mother and had a powerful experience of Christ on Good Friday, but after returning to Ireland, she went back to her partying. Drunk and vomiting one night, she heard the words, *Why do you continue to hurt me?* Clare realized then that her life would have no meaning apart from Christ. Ignoring the pleas of her manager and family, she entered the Sisters' community in Spain in 2001.

As a religious sister, always with a guitar in hand, Sister Clare spent time working with and teaching the poor in various cities in Spain, Florida, and Ecuador. Her exuberant love for others came from Jesus in the Eucharist. She wrote, "Inside the church is the tabernacle and in the tabernacle, the Eucharist. Hardly anyone goes there to visit Our Lord. Sometimes, during the day, I sneak away to that little village. I rest my forehead against the tabernacle and keep the Lord company for a while, which does me SO MUCH GOOD."[52]

In 2016, Sister Clare was serving in her community's poor village school in Ecuador. One evening, she and ten companions (two other sisters and eight young women) were cleaning up after a day of classes. Suddenly, an earthquake hit. Sister Clare and five young women were killed. Her story went viral on the internet and touched millions of people because of the vivacious way she had lived—always united to Jesus in the Eucharist, communicating love to everyone she encountered. Jesus had communicated to her his desire for her life, and she had responded with her witness of a communicative love.

Sister Clare used her music and joyful spirit to communicate Jesus' love. We, too, share in Christ's Eucharistic communication when we communicate his love to others, online or in-person. Each human being also becomes a communication of Christ's love for us.

Today, reflect on how you can be a Eucharistic presence for others you engage with online. Spend a little time with Jesus present in the tabernacle of a Catholic church or chapel. Let your conversation with him be an intimate communication of love.

*Jesus, present in the Eucharist, let me recognize how much you love me in giving yourself to me as food. I want to appreciate this great mystery that is the greatest of mass communication media and go to you often to be nourished, transformed, and renewed. Help me to share in your communication of love in the media culture.*

WEEK 6 SATURDAY
# Spiritual Transformation

Do not be conformed to this world, but be transformed by the renewing of your minds, so that you may discern what is the will of God—what is good and acceptable and perfect.

*—Romans 12:2*

WE'VE BEEN ON THIS spiritual journey for the past six weeks. Perhaps we have found ourselves stumbling through the fasting experience, alternating between confidence and weariness. Yet, all along God's grace has transformed us, sometimes imperceptibly. Today let's reflect on how this experience will change our lives and media use going forward.

Transformations are standard fare in popular storytelling. Some heroes make a heel turn and become villains, while certain antagonists turn good. Characters' development often culminates in increased strength or a loss of control. Some transformations are external, while others affect the inner character. These transformations symbolize the workings of grace in us.

Kylo Ren in the *Star Wars* sequel trilogy wreaks havoc in the galaxy by turning to the dark side. He tries to manipulate the new Jedi, Rey, to join him in his murderous rage, but she refuses. Though he desires to prove himself evil, his encounter with Rey draws out the best of his humanity. In a desperate moment when Rey calls for help, Kylo turns from his followers and saves Rey's life by sacrificing his own. In a profound redemptive moment of grace, Kylo, also known as Ben Solo, discovers his true self and ultimately aids the survival of the Rebellion.

God wants us to discover our true selves in him. He loves us no matter who we are. Even when we sin, he pours his mercy upon us, desiring our return to his embrace. Jesus, perfectly God and perfectly human, shows us what true humanity looks like through surrender to the Father's will. The moments we choose to follow his will in our lives are the moments when we are the most Christ-like. This transformative union with Christ happens gradually as we daily make the decision to follow him.

Reviewing the experience of this fast, we may notice how God's grace opens us to greater trust. Our security lies less in our media connectedness and more in the power of his grace. This reality gives us confidence, for we know that we are not alone on the journey and that we have the strength to choose the good life, to be cultural mystics who transform the culture by the way we live.

Focus your prayer today on surrendering to God's transformative grace in your life. Go forth from this fasting experience renewed, refreshed, and transformed to live well with your media.

*Heavenly Father, your grace enlightens and transforms me the more I seek to do your will. Fill me with strength and courage to make good media choices so as to live a happy and fulfilled life in union with you.*

# Media Fast Check-in

You made it to the end of this fasting challenge. What did you learn about yourself? How did this fast affect your relationship with Jesus?

## Prayer in Reparation for the Misuse of the Media

*Heavenly Father, thank you for the opportunity to influence the media culture for good through my efforts during this spiritual journey. Have mercy on those who perpetrate polarization or violence through their media creations. May my media use inspire others to be communicators of love and unity, as I seek to transform the culture for Christ. Amen.*

## You Did It

Making the decision to embark on a spiritual quest is half the battle. Completing this fast is a major accomplishment. Now we go forward, allowing the changes we made in our relationship with our media to help us use media well for the good of our whole selves.

> Life is a great journey toward eternity, and each day is a stage of that journey.[53]

—Blessed James Alberione

## Life Hack for the Week

Consider one fruit you gained from this media fast. Write out a plan for how you will continue to make room for that fruit of grace to grow in your life. Put it on your mirror so you see it when you wake up and when you go to bed.

# CONCLUSION

# Moving Forward with My Media

Small changes make for capital, and the attentive person gains treasures for heaven.[54]

—*Blessed James Alberione*

CONGRATULATIONS! WE FINISHED OUR media fast!

As we conclude, we may notice how blessed we can feel when living the present moment without all the distractions of our screens. Some of our blessings may be a decrease in anxiety from lessening our screen use or an increase of joy from hanging out in-person with friends and family. Other blessings may be seeing how sharing positivity online breeds joy, or how respecting someone through our kind response to a heated post circulates charity. Living intentionally with our media increases our ability to appreciate the beauty before us and all around us both within and outside of our media use.

We may also have noticed that being mindful of how we use our media can help us live with greater awareness of the gift of time—which Jean-Pierre de Caussade calls "the sacrament of the present moment"—allowing us to better hear the voice of God as he speaks to us in the everyday circumstances of life. Each day has its own trials, so we can only attend to the present, leaving the past to God's mercy and the future to his Provident care.

Now the spiritual journey continues. This book is a starting point for us to balance our relationship with media so that it enhances our life instead of diminishing it. These reflections are a launching pad for a deeper encounter and friendship with Christ. The awareness of Christ's presence working in our daily media experience can make us more intentional about our media choices moving forward.

You created a plan for your digital fast; now you can use the lessons you learned to create a new strategy to move forward with your media. This will help you to center your media on Christ by taking the insights and growth of your fast into your everyday life.

———————————————————————— ∞∞ ————————————————————————

## What I learned

1. What did I like most about the fast?

2. What did this fast teach me about the ways I use media?

3. What was the hardest moment and what did it tell me about myself?

## 4. What surprised me about myself during this fast?

5. How did my relationship with God change during this
   fast?

6. What did I learn about the relationship between God and media?

## 7. What will I take away from this experience?

8. What obstacles did I face? What worked or didn't work to overcome those obstacles?

## Looking Ahead

1. What would I like my relationship to media to be now and in the future? What will I do to make that a reality?

2. What behaviors practiced during this fast do I want
   to integrate into my daily life? How can I incorporate
   them now that the fast is over?

3. Are there any elements of the fast that I will continue
   to do each day?

4. How can I make my relationship with Christ central in my digital experience? How will I change my priorities to make this a reality?

## Predict obstacles

| Obstacles that may arise: | Ways I will respond to each obstacle: |
|---|---|
|  |  |
|  |  |
|  |  |
|  |  |

# Spirituality for a Digital Age

The Holy Spirit transforms us. With our cooperation, he wants to transform the world we live in.[55]

—*Pope Francis*

THIS BOOK NOT ONLY specifies skills for critical engagement with the media, but also facilitates a way of praying with, for, and in the popular media culture. A media spirituality starts with the belief that all instruments of communication are gifts of God. Using these media well depends on our discerned and reflective choices. When we contemplate the popular culture and recognize the needs of humanity expressed in the media, we can bring them to prayer. In the Appendices, there are specific prayers, practices, and ways of praying the media that can assist us on this journey.

This book doesn't have to be a one-time read. It could be a resource we turn to often, especially when we need a digital detox. My hope is that these tools and reflections may become a guide to living an intimate relationship with Jesus Christ while navigating our digital world.

Now let's go live our faith and our media experience with commitment, sacrifice, intentionality, and radical responsibility!

# Acknowledgments

THE AUTHOR AND PAULINE Books & Media gratefully acknowledge the following sources from which excerpts appear in this book:

Papal and magisterial texts copyright © Dicastero per la Comunicazione-Libreria Editrice Vaticana. All rights reserved. Used with permission.

Excerpts from the English translation of the *Catechism of the Catholic Church* for use in the United States of America, copyright © 1994, United States Catholic Conference, Inc.—Libreria Editrice Vaticana. Modifications from the Editio Typica copyright © 1997, United States Conference of Catholic Bishops—Libreria Editrice Vaticana. Used with permission.

Excerpts from *Brevi Meditazione Per Ogni Giorno dell'Anno*, copyright © 2008, *Ut Perfectus Sit Homo Dei*, copyright © 1998, *Notes in Pastoral Theology*, copyright © 2001, by Blessed James Alberione, Edizioni San Paolo, Rome. All rights reserved.

Excerpts from *The Following of Christ the Master, Looking at Christ the Master, Announcing Christ the Master*, by Blessed James Alberione, copyright © n.d., Daughters of St. Paul, Boston, MA. All rights reserved.

Excerpts from *Thoughts: Fragments of Apostolic Spirituality from his Writings and Talks*, by Blessed James Alberione (tr. Aloysius Milella), copyright © 1974, Daughters of St. Paul, Boston, MA. All rights reserved.

# Appendix A

# Media Addictions

Behavioral addictions associated with technology have become a growing problem in our culture. Knowing how to spot these addictions, when to seek help, how to overcome them, and how faith supports the healing process can be helpful, whether media addiction becomes an issue for us or for someone we know.

A war veteran suffering from PTSD ended up hospitalized after playing countless hours of *Call of Duty*. A young woman used social media for work and personal interactions but became so preoccupied with FOMO that she entertained dark thoughts about whether anyone even cared about her at all.

For many people, media use is non-problematic. But more than 6 percent of the world population meets the criteria for compulsive or excessive technology use that can lead to addiction.[56] Technology or internet addiction is generally manifested as a loss of control of internet usage regardless of its harmful consequences.[57] Media addiction has not been classified as a disorder in the *Diagnostic and Statistical Manual of Mental Disorders* (DSM-5) from the American Psychiatric Association, yet the criteria for recognizing excessive media use are similar to the criteria for other addictions: compulsive behavior and diminishment of the ability to perform daily tasks.

Various psychological issues are related not only to *how much time* we spend on technology but also *how we use* media. There are several types of internet disorders associated with use of media: cybersex or pornography; excessive online gambling; and compulsive use of video games, online messaging, social media, and online shopping. Other media disorders can result from binge-watching shows, ceaselessly listening to music, or spending a disproportionate amount of time reading books, magazines, and comic series.[58] Like substance abuse, some media addictions affect the reward center of our brain. Constant scrolling on social media or seeking rewards in games activates neural pathways that produce a chemical rush of positive reinforcement. Dopamine-inducing media sites absorb our attention.

An excessive concern with and uncontrolled urge for technology use may be a sign of addiction, especially when these behaviors lead to withdrawal from real-life relationships and responsibilities or lack of attention to physical health. When this urge becomes a debilitating, constant drive, it can impair a person's functions in everyday life and lead to pathological issues[59] such as depression, anxiety, and loss of life interests.

## Technology Addiction Assessment

Here are some questions you can ask yourself about your relationship to media:[60]

- Do I find myself spending hours with my media when I intended to spend only a few minutes?
- Do I set limits for my media use but find myself ignoring the time limit?
- Do I binge media late into the night?
- Do I compulsively reach for my devices when I have a free moment?
- Do I neglect my physical health, hygiene, or nutrition because of compulsive media use?
- Am I sad, depressed, or anxious when not using my media?

- Have my relationships suffered because of my media use?
- Are other aspects of my life (work, studies, finances) suffering as a result of my compulsive media use?
- Do I lie to others about how much time I spend with my media or the content I consume?
- Do I feel ashamed about my excessive media use?

If you answered "yes" to several of these questions, you may have a technology disorder. The good news is that many people can detach themselves from excessive media use by a significant reduction of their screen time through a digital fast or detox.

Getting through a media fast, however, is just the beginning. We don't want to return to our old habits when the fast is complete. Instead, we can use the section "Moving Forward with My Media" to create a plan for how to live well with our media. More moderate usage and accountability to a particular person can help us take charge of our media use.

## Faith and Healing

Faith and spirituality can support healing and recovery from technology disorders and addictions. Prayer, meditation, and silent reflection, in addition to professional mental health assistance, are crucial for integrating our spiritual lives with our emotional and physical well-being.

Developing a relationship with Jesus, Way, Truth, and Life, facilitates personal integration. In dialogue with Christ, we discover the truths of ourselves in light of the One who is Truth Itself; we recognize when our choices are for the good of our whole selves and others, and we seek the life of freedom that Christ offers to us.

The best way to nurture our relationship with Jesus is through the sacraments of the Catholic Church. Every time we receive the sacraments of Reconciliation and Eucharist, we receive the gift of God himself and the grace to continue our journey of life with greater strength of conviction and hope in his love. The sacraments heal and nourish our souls, giving us the ability to resist the temptation to turn to technology as a crutch for our emotional needs. Instead, Jesus waits for us to open ourselves to him, for he loves us infinitely. He will always take care of us in his way and in his time, for he knows what is best for us, more than we do ourselves.

Technology addictions are treatable just like other addictions. However, they do require persistence and self-discipline. We can do it! We are beautiful in the eyes of God, who desires our wholeness and happiness. Let us allow Christ to look upon us with his merciful, life-giving gaze that generates saints. In and through his love, we grow in holiness, are healed of our sins, and receive the grace to overcome our weaknesses. In Christ alone we find hope to begin again living the life he desires for us.

## Resources

It is important to find support if you experience anxiety with your media use or repeatedly fall back into problematic behaviors even after a time of fasting. If you notice unwarranted feelings of sadness, fatigue, depression, helplessness, or irritability, or if you have thoughts of suicide, you may have a serious addiction and need to seek immediate professional help.

Here are some resources for professional assistance:

**Omega Recovery (omegarecovery.org)** is an accredited mental health provider specializing in technology addictions. It was founded by Dr. Nicholas Kardaras, who is the United States' foremost digital addiction expert. It provides online and outpatient services through hotlines and individual case management and inpatient assistance for a more integral recovery.

**Media Addicts Anonymous (mediaaddictsanonymous.org)** is a peer group that meets virtually, using the twelve-step recovery process. Though they are not affiliated with any religion, the organization encourages a relationship with God, community, and personal responsibility as means to overcome addiction. Internet and Technology Addicts Anonymous (internetaddictsanonymous. org) similarly uses the twelve-step process.

**Catholic in Recovery (catholicinrecovery.com)** is a non-profit organization that serves those who seek recovery from all types of addictions. It specializes in the twelve-step process to lead people to recovery along with sacramental grace provided by the Catholic Church. By providing parishes with resources, the organization aims to assure those struggling that God can bring about healing and recovery, even in the most desperate cases.

**Catholic Counselors (catholiccounselors.com)** is a telehealth multi-faceted mental health and pastoral counseling service offering assistance for behavior addictions with an attention to personal growth and spiritual development.

# APPENDIX B

# Pornography

WE ARE MADE FOR intimacy—a beautiful gift. The human person is created in the image and likeness of God. The human body and intimate relationships are expressions of the divine artistry. Every human being is created to love and be loved. In a sexual relationship within marriage, love involves the mind, body, soul, and spirit of the person. Connecting with another person in this way provides spiritual, physical, and psychological fulfillment. Through spousal love we become a gift to one another. Saint John Paul II says:

> The human body . . . contains "from the beginning" the "spousal" attribute, that is, *the power to express love: precisely that love in which the human person becomes a gift* and—through this gift—fulfills the very meaning of his being and existence.[61]

Pornography and masturbation lack the components of a spousal relationship (mind, body, soul, spirit, and love) and remove intimacy from sex. The human person is seen as only a commodity used for personal pleasure. The sexual pleasure sought removes the possibility of lasting fulfillment that we find in committed relationships, because self-gift is missing.

Porn seriously harms the one using it and the one exploited by it because it is an offense against the human dignity of both the user and the used. It ignores the responsibility we have to uphold the dignity of every person, and it destroys the sense of the user's dignity. To paraphrase Saint John Paul II's seminal *Theology of the Body*, when the human person is objectified, the body and soul are seen as separate and dignity is removed. This is why pornography is a problem. It shows through the exposed image or video not too much of the person, but too little.[62]

Pornography is not just a private issue. It exploits other human beings and alters how one interacts with others: it can cause communication problems, emotional distancing, mental health issues, sexual and physical abuse, and other disorders.[63] The addition of pornography in a marriage doubles the likelihood of divorce[64] because it creates a disconnect from real relationships.

The types of sex acts shown in pornography can normalize unhealthy sexual practices that are often degrading to women in particular and can lead to sexual aggression. Researchers have discovered a direct connection between porn use and sex trafficking, child molestation, trivialization of rape, and increased sexual violence.[65] Viewing porn can lead to unhealthy expectations within sexual relationships when viewers or their partners develop body image issues as a result of comparing their bodies to those of the actors in internet porn, or when they or their partners are expected to duplicate the extreme violent sexual practices seen in porn, even when one partner is uncomfortable.

The late Dr. Al Cooper noted several factors that draw people to engage in internet porn. He referred to them as the triple "A" influence: accessibility, affordability, and anonymity.[66] Personal digital devices make it easy to be secretive, and an internet connection allows for instant access to loads of free porn sites. The intoxicating nature and easy accessibility of internet porn makes addiction more possible.

Strong neuroscientific evidence shows that internet pornography is highly addictive[67] and desensitizes viewers to real pleasure. Many men and women who engage in porn and masturbate have less desire and pleasure in their sexual relationships. Like other addictions, pornography carves out neural pathways in the brain, increasing desire while decreasing satisfaction. But even if someone may not be seriously addicted to porn, any amount of porn use is harmful.

In addition to physical and psychological harm, the Catechism reminds us that pornography use and masturbation are morally harmful actions.[68] If we are enslaved by these sins, we can be set free through a conversion to faith in Christ and especially in his mercy.

## Faith in Christ

A relationship with Jesus is the antidote to porn.[69] It strengthens us in the knowledge that we are made in God's image, that God does not create anything but what is beautiful and restores the innocence and beauty lost by our sins. God loves us immensely and desires our healing. We can remove the lies we've believed about ourselves—that we are unattractive, unworthy, or unlovable—or the lies about our porn use—that it's not hurting anyone, that we can quit anytime, or that we can never break free of the addiction. Our relationship with Jesus leads us to know the truth that we are created to be self-gift, since he shows us that it is in giving that we receive. Nothing can replace the love we have to offer the world. In Christ, we live fully in the Father's loving embrace, and through that love we shine light upon everyone we encounter.

Being centered in Christ also helps us to see the goodness and dignity of others. Many of Jesus' teachings focus on how we treat our fellow human beings—"Love your neighbor as yourself" (Mk 12:31), "Do to others as you would have them do to you" (Lk 6:31), "Be merciful, just as your Father is merciful" (Lk 6:36). Jesus emphasizes that loving others involves respect for their dignity, as shown in the way he spent time with tax collectors, prostitutes, and sinners to teach them the ways of God. Jesus calls us to make choices that support the dignity and integrity of ourselves and others when he says, "Just as I have loved you, you also should love one another" (Jn 13:34).

Like any addiction, we can't overcome porn addiction alone. When we bring it to our relationship with Jesus, his mercy, grace, and love pour upon us. Prayer and surrender to his grace help us realize we are not in control and need him to enable us to overcome the strong urges to use porn. True freedom comes when we learn to receive the love and mercy of Christ, our Savior; when we learn to depend on him and recognize that he is the one who is capable of meeting all our needs and satisfying all our desires. True freedom also requires that we seek the help of other people to hold us accountable and to not give up on us when we fall. The Catechism speaks of chastity as a virtue that requires an *"apprenticeship in self-mastery."*[70] Finding mentors and counselors to accompany us in the journey is essential to overcoming porn addiction so that, when faced with the temptation to use porn, we can choose life, love, and true freedom in Christ.

## Resources

If you find that you engage with porn, there are resources to help you overcome this destructive habit. God created you to be a gift to others and to respect yourself and others as gift. To live out your call as gift, it's necessary that you detox from pornography by removing it completely from your life. That includes identifying and addressing triggers that lead you to seek release in porn. For example, if there are forms of media that lead you to engage in using porn, you should eliminate those media as well. If your addiction is severe, then you most likely need professional assistance. Additionally, if relational difficulties or sexual trauma have affected your life and influenced your experience with pornography or masturbation, a therapist who is trained in sexual addiction and trauma would be most helpful.

Here are some resources to help with recovery and growth in an integrated sexuality:

**Covenant Eyes (covenanteyes.com)** offers a wholistic approach to freedom from porn with multimedia options to keep oneself accountable. Scripturally based, it provides numerous free resources for oneself or for loved ones and more behind a paywall. There are women-specific resources as well as those for faith leaders.

**Center for Healing (centerforhealingkc.com)** is a Catholic-based organization providing professional counseling in-person and virtually in states where its therapists are certified. Individual virtual coaching is also available, along with a three-day intensive workshop for men struggling with pornography and unwanted sexual behaviors, to offer a wholistic approach by addressing each person's physical, emotional, and spiritual needs.

**Magdala Ministries (magdalaministries.org)** accompanies women with sexual addictions, specifically pornography addictions. Through virtual groups around the world, and by partnering with Catholic parishes for in-person groups, this organization guides women on the path of healing and hope. For a one-time fee, participants are connected with a group and receive the curriculum.

**Integrity Restored (integrityrestored.com)** is a Catholic diocesan-based online site to help individuals and families affected by pornography regain integrity. Providing education, training, and encouragement, this site helps people break free from addiction and heal relationships so that the domestic church can be restored to being the place of encountering Christ.

**Fortify (joinfortify.com)** is a non-religious site that assists with recovery from porn addiction and bringing about lasting change. The site emphasizes connecting with others through fellowship and creating supportive communities. This site also offers resources for those assisting someone in recovery.

**Sexaholics Anonymous (sa.org)** follows the twelve-step process to lead members to recovery from sexual addiction. Through localized meetings, regional events, and national conventions, those who struggle with addiction find fellowship and continual support.

**Catholic Counselors (catholiccounselors.com)** is a telehealth multi-faceted mental health and pastoral counseling service offering assistance for behavior addictions with an attention to personal growth and spiritual development.

# Appendix C

# Prayers

## Prayer to Be Media Mindful

Spirit of Wisdom, you breathe life into humanity to discover and create technologies that promote global communication through the sharing of information and entertainment. These gifts of God give expression to the desires and yearnings of humanity through the art of popular culture.

Teach us to engage mindfully with the media, discovering the seeds of grace present there, while seeking to understand the needs of humanity today, always ready to propose Christ as the fulfiller of all our hopes and longings.

Assist us with your grace, O Divine Spirit! Help us to use these means to discern the signs of the times, to search for a Christian response, and to derive motives for prayer.

We ask this through the perfect Communicator, Jesus our Master and Lord. Amen.

*By the Daughters of St. Paul*

# Canticle of Praise for the Media in Today's World

May you be praised, Lord God, for the printed word, bread for our minds, light for our lives.

We give thanks for the dedication of all who serve the truth in love, and for all whose technical and professional skills make possible the production of books, newspapers, magazines, and reviews.

We celebrate, Lord, the modern marvel of television, which brings into the heart of our homes the joy and the pain of all human living. Music, drama, and laughter are shared in ways undreamed of in the past.

May you be praised, Lord God, for the radio, which soars on the wings of the wind and provides for each nation an immediate channel for news, views, and entertainment, and a means of offering to the listening world its own distinctive voice.

We celebrate, Lord, the writers, directors, and all those whose gifts light both theater and cinema and provide audiences with a heightened awareness of their human condition.

We celebrate the wonder of digital communications, which manifests a new iconography that links people around the globe in solidarity of faith, hope, and love.

We thank you, Lord God, for the unending Pentecost of your creative Holy Spirit, which enables your sons and daughters to be afire with your truth, beauty, and goodness.

May the blind see, the deaf hear, and the poor receive justice through the proclamation of the Good News via today's media.

Together let us rejoice in the God-given talents and creative gifts of those who promote the dignity of the human person and who build communion among peoples the world over through their dedication and love. Amen.

*Based on the writings of Blessed James Alberione, SSP*

## Proclaiming Christ through the Media Arts

Lord of all our hopes, you are the Living One who conquered death and sent your Spirit to renew all things. You guide the way of all men and women who journey through history, and you sustain the commitment of all those who participate in the creative work of renewing the universe.

We offer you, Lord, the joys and successes of all your children committed to the various fields of media.

We present their constant search for you so that they may proclaim you in truth, justice, freedom, and love. Lord, guide those who use the various media arts to open new horizons of hope, of true life, of solidarity, of communication, and of communion. With hope we look forward to a new world, which you call us to build through our work as evangelizers.

We pray that our efforts may contribute to building a world of peace and unity. God of salvation, love, and hope, enfold all who search for you in your most tender embrace. Amen.

*By the Daughters of St. Paul*

## Litany of Media Saints for Media Mindfulness

Most Holy Trinity, Father, Son, and Holy Spirit, your inner life of love is the essence of our communion. Have mercy on us.

Mary, Queen of Apostles, you help us respect the dignity of every human person and reflect that dignity in the media we produce and consume. Pray for us.

Saint Gabriel, you brought God's invitation to Mary and announced that Jesus would save us from our sins; you who are the patron of radio, telecommunications, and communication workers, pray for us.

Saint Paul, you are the apostle who proclaimed Christ to all peoples through your preaching, example, and letters; you who are the patron saint of the Catholic press and a patron of writers, pray for us.

Saint Cecilia, you loved Jesus above all things and brought joy to your friends and family in the faith through beautiful sounds; you who are the patron of music and musicians, pray for us.

Saint Bernardine of Siena, you proclaimed Jesus to everyone you met; you spread devotion to the Eucharist and the Holy Name of Jesus; you created a logo for Jesus' name and are the patron of those who work in public relations; pray for us.

Saint Clare, you loved Jesus and dedicated your whole life to him and the Church as a nun; you saw the Mass appear on your wall when you were too sick to attend; you who are the patron saint of television, television workers, and all those who watch television, pray for us.

Saint Genesius, you who once mocked the Christian faith as a comedian and actor; you who were converted when acting in a play about Baptism, and are the patron saint of actors, pray for us.

Saint Francis de Sales, you wrote many books about loving God and how to live the spiritual life; you who are the patron saint of journalists and the good press, pray for us.

Saint Luke the Evangelist and Saint Catherine of Alexandria, you loved art and gave us images of what is true, good, and beautiful; you who are the patrons of artists, pray for us.

Saint Martin de Porres, Saint Mary Magdalen, and Venerable Pierre Toussaint, you who are the patrons of hairdressers and therefore those who create special effects in media, pray for us.

Saint Isidore of Seville, you wrote the world's first "database" of information. You who are the patron of the internet, pray for us.

Saint Albert the Great, you are the patron saint of science and technology. Pray for all those who use science and technology to communicate information and entertainment stories to us, and pray for us.

Saint Thomas Aquinas, you were a great thinker and philosopher; because of your great faith, there was never any question of which you were afraid. Give us the wisdom to always ask questions of the media so we can be mindful of media messages, and pray for us.

Saint Maximilian Kolbe, you discovered the power of the radio to proclaim the truth of the human person and were imprisoned in Auschwitz for preaching against the Nazi regime. You who are the patron of amateur radio operators and radio stations, pray for us.

Blessed James Alberione, you saw every media invention as a "gift of God" to be used by the Church to evangelize the culture. You are considered the "media apostle of the new evangelization." We pray that you will one day be named patron of all the media; pray for us.

Blessed Carlo Acutis, you who were a gamer and computer programmer, creating a website to document Eucharistic miracles from around the world, inspire all who work in computer science and information systems, that they may use these technologies to uplift the human spirit. You who may one day be named patron of programmers, coders, and gamers, pray for us.

All Saints, you once lived among us and witnessed to the love of Christ for everyone in your own times. We live now in a media world. Show us the way to make thoughtful choices about the media so that we may find Jesus in our daily lives. Help us to become media mindful. Pray for us.

*By the Daughters of St. Paul*

## A Prayer to Discern the Cries of Humanity in Popular Music

Lord Jesus,
you incarnated yourself in our world,
taking on our flesh and expressing yourself through our culture and language.
Help us to be discerning listeners of music today.
May we take notice of the deeper longings expressed there

for love, hope, peace, and meaning.
Make our hearts compassionate to the pains and struggles of
    others,
especially those who are different from us.
Teach us how to find the seeds of the Gospel you have plant-
    ed in the popular culture,
and to nurture these seeds lovingly,
separating out the good from the bad
and holding fast to what is good (cf. 1 Thess 5:21).
May your grace abound in the hearts of all who hear this
    music,
and in the hearts of those who make it.
We ask this, Jesus, in your name. Amen.

*By the Daughters of St. Paul*

# Appendix D

# Practices

## Examination of Conscience for My Online Life

How do I practice balance in my online life?

Is my internet use put at the service of the common good? If so, how? If not, what do I need to change?

Do I respect other people and their opinions?

Does my online activity move toward helping myself and others grow in virtue?

Does my online presence reflect my authentic self, or do I try to hide behind a false persona?

What are some of my current online behaviors that I need to re-evaluate? Do I engage in pornography?

Are there other challenges I face in my online life? How might I practically address them?

Might I benefit from talking about my online challenges with someone: a trusted friend, family member, or confessor?

Lord, forgive me for my failings and sins in my use of digital technology. I recognize the need to change my online behaviors to grow in my relationship with you and to live a life of virtue involving balance and reason. I desire to be more attentive to your presence while online. Help me to be kind, respectful, and loving of everyone I engage with online, remembering that they are human beings with feelings and emotions. Lord, I resolve to be your digital disciple who witnesses to your grace at work in my life through the media with which I engage. Amen.

*By the Daughters of St. Paul*

Fasting from our media involves not only removal of problematic media; it also includes replacing the time spent with technology with in-person spiritual and corporal works of mercy. We can put into practice what Jesus says: "Be merciful, just as your Father is merciful" (Lk 6:36).

## Spiritual Works of Mercy

Instruct the ignorant.

Counsel the doubtful.

Admonish the sinner.

Patiently bear with those who wrong us.

Forgive offenses.

Comfort the afflicted.

Pray for the living and the dead.

## Corporal Works of Mercy

Feed the hungry.

Give water to the thirsty.

Shelter the homeless.

Clothe the naked.

Visit the sick.

Visit the imprisoned.

Bury the dead.

## Cinema Divina

*Cinema divina* draws on the ancient prayer form of *lectio divina*. Unlike film discussions, *cinema divina* is more of a prayer experience than a conversation, although there is an element of sharing involved. This is more effective when done in a group, but it can be adapted for personal prayer and reflection.

**Lectio**: Begin with a prayer to the Holy Spirit. Read a Scripture passage that connects to the theme of the movie. View the film; then re-read the Scripture.

**Meditatio**: Invite each person present to share briefly what part of the film or Scripture stood out to them. This is not necessarily their favorite part of the film, but the part God is inviting them to explore.

**Oratio**: Go around the room again and invite each person to offer a short prayer based on their reflection.

**Contemplatio**: The leader allows a few moments of silence for each person to bring to personal prayer what stood out to them from the Scripture and film.

**Actio**: Go around the room a last time and invite each person to share a concrete action they feel inspired to do as a result of their reflection.

End the *cinema divina* with a closing prayer, such as the Our Father or one of your own composition.

Note: *Cinema divina* movie guides for many popular films are available for download at pauline.org/media-studies-resources.

*By the Daughters of St. Paul*

# Praying the News

Sometimes we are overwhelmed by the problems of the world and are unsure of what we can do. Intercessory prayer for others puts our own troubles into perspective and allows us to offer all to God. Using the daily news as a springboard for prayer can help us be more aware of what is happening in the world around us while presenting these petitions to our merciful and loving God, asking him to heal the world from all the sin and strife.

Praying the news is a simple practice that leads us to pray for the needs of the world and also for the media outlets that present the news. Here is an outline you may find helpful to follow.

1. Begin with an opening prayer:

> Lord, I check the news every day, and every day I am shocked and saddened, but also inspired and encouraged.
>
> As I take in the news today, dear Lord, inspire me to pray for those involved in the stories, those affected by the events, and all who announce and receive the news. Give me the gift of awareness and a sense of responsibility, especially toward the most vulnerable in our society and in our world.
>
> Expand my heart, Lord, and give me a share of your love, that I may embrace all that is news today. Amen.

2. Next, experience the news in whatever format you choose. If you are praying with a group, viewing television news or online news works best. Any number of 24-hour news channels or online streaming sites would work.

3. After viewing or reading the news, spend a few moments in quiet contemplation, letting your heart absorb the news stories you experienced.

4. Pray for the people involved in the news stories you read or heard.

If you are in a group, the leader can invite participants to express their intercessory prayer out loud. Pray or sing a refrain after every two or three intercessions.

5. Whether praying alone or together, bring the intercession to a close by praying the Our Father.

6. End with a closing prayer.

*By the Daughters of St. Paul*

## Novena of Prayer for Celebrities

When you like a celebrity, you might follow that person's work, or follow him or her on social media. You might even try to meet your favorite celebrity one day at a concert, conference, or convention, or get a picture together if you see him or her at an event. Praying for a particular celebrity we admire puts our adulation in perspective and helps us see celebrities as human beings with the same struggles and challenges as the rest of humanity. It also recognizes their need for prayer, since they have a responsibility to promote the good, the true, and the beautiful in their craft and since their lives are always in the media for everyone to see. We pray for these iconic personalities to be respectful, loving, and holy individuals and so offer good example to all. Even if you never meet your favorite celebrities, you are connected to them through prayer. You can lift them up to God and intercede for them.

Here is the process of praying for a particular celebrity:

1. Think of one of your favorite celebrities. It could be an actor, singer, musician, dancer, TV show host, artist, athlete, politician, comedian, famous chef . . . any celebrity you like and admire.

2. Consider this person as a real person with likes and dislikes, with wonderful qualities and faults, with talents and limitations, with personal joys and struggles. Have you ever noticed or thought

about what some of these might be? Have you ever brought these to God for that person?

3. On a small piece of paper, write down the name of your celebrity or the celebrity that God is placing on your heart to pray for right now.

4. Write out a prayer for your celebrity. Include an element of thanksgiving (thanking God for the life, talent, inspiration, etc. of the person) and an element of petition (interceding for a particular need of this celebrity, or a hope that this person has for his or her life, or asking that this person come closer to God, etc.).

5. Pray with your written prayer quietly (1–2 minutes of silence).

6. Pray this prayer as a novena: each day for a nine-day stretch.

*By the Daughters of St. Paul*

# About Pauline Media Studies

## Media mindfulness catechesis for lived discipleship

Pauline Media Studies is a project of the Daughters of Saint Paul, women religious dedicated to live Christ's life and communicate Christ's presence with the media and in the media culture. The Center's focus is to develop and encourage media mindfulness in areas of faith formation, education, and culture. We do this by teaching the skills to critically analyze media messages through the lens of Gospel values to form missionary disciples who engage in the digital culture.cffr

The Center develops a theology of popular culture and of communications while contributing to the Church's understanding of herself within the media culture. It offers a model of catechesis that integrates media literacy within an understanding of the faith lived in the everyday popular media experience. All the works of the Center are infused with a media spirituality, which is the Pauline spirituality developed by Blessed James Alberione, founder of the Pauline Family. His vision was to influence the media culture by bringing Christ the Master, Way, Truth, and Life to the heart of human living after the example of Saint Paul the Apostle.

The Center promotes media mindfulness catechesis through in-person and online classes, media mindfulness workshops, blog articles, film and TV reviews, media retreats, *cinema divina* events, Scriptural movie guides, and much more.

Visit the website at: pauline.org/media-studies-resources and find ways to bring Christ into your media experience.

# Notes

1. James Alberione, *Brevi meditazioni per ogni giorno dell'anno,* trans. Carmen Pompei, FSP (Roma: Edizioni San Paolo, 2008), 167.

2. James Alberione, *The Following of Christ the Master, Looking at Christ the Master, Announcing Christ the Master* (Boston: Daughters of St. Paul, n.d.), 123.

3. Pope Francis, "Message of His Holiness Pope Francis for Lent 2022," para. 9, https://www.vatican.va/content/francesco/en/messages/lent/documents/20211111-messaggio-quaresima2022.html.

4. James Alberione, *Thoughts: Fragments of Apostolic Spirituality from His Writings and Talks,* trans. Aloysius Milella (Boston: St. Paul Editions, 1974), 38.

5. Alberione, *Thoughts,* 38.

6. Pope Francis, "Homily of His Holiness Pope Francis," Ash Wednesday, March 6, 2019, https://www.vatican.va/content/francesco/en/homilies/2019/documents/papa-francesco_20190306_omelia-ceneri.html.

7. "Anxiety Disorders—Facts & Statistics," Anxiety & Depression Association of America, accessed February 5, 2024, https://adaa.org/understanding-anxiety/facts-statistics.

8. "2022 Annual Report," Anxiety Canada, accessed February 5, 2024, https://www.anxietycanada.com/wp-content/uploads/2023/04/2022-Annual-Impact-Report.pdf.

9. Luca Braghieri, Ro'ee Levy, and Alexey Makarin, "Social Media and Mental Health," last revised August 22, 2023, available at SSRN: https://ssrn.com/abstract=3919760.

10. https://www.globaldayofunplugging.org/.

11. James Alberione, *Ut Perfectus Sit Homo Dei*, trans. Mike Byrnes (Rome: Edizioni San Paolo, 1998), 19.

12. Alberione, *Thoughts*, 40.

13. "Pornography Statistics," Covenant Eyes, https://www.covenanteyes.com/pornstats/.

14. Arina O. Grossu and Sean Maguire, "The Link Between Pornography, Sex Trafficking, and Abortion," Family Research Council, November 2017, https://downloads.frc.org/EF/EF17K24.pdf.

15. "Porn in the Digital Age: New Research Reveals 10 Trends," Barna Group, April 6, 2016, https://www.barna.com/research/porn-in-the-digital-age-new-research-reveals-10-trends/.

16. Gary Wilson, *Your Brain on Porn: Internet Pornography and the Emerging Science of Addiction*, 2nd ed. (UK: Commonwealth Publishing, 2017).

17. Grossu and Maguire, "The Link Between Pornography . . ."

18. See John Paul II, *Man and Woman He Created Them: A Theology of the Body* (Boston: Pauline Books & Media, 2006), 349–52.

19. *Catechism of the Catholic Church*, 2nd ed. (Huntington, IN: Our Sunday Visitor, 1997), no. 2338.

20. Emily A. Vogels, "The State of Online Harassment," Pew Research, January 13, 2021, https://www.pewresearch.org/internet/2021/01/13/the-state-of-online-harassment/.

21. *Ted Lasso*, season 1, episode 8, "The Diamond Dogs," directed by Declan Lowney, written by Leann Bowen, featuring Jason Sudeikis and Hannah Waddingham, aired September 18, 2020, on AppleTV+.

22. *Ted Lasso*, season 1, episode 8, "The Diamond Dogs."

23. Alberione, *Thoughts*, 36.

24. Alberione, *Thoughts*, 170.

25. Gretchen Hailer, Thomas Zanizig, and Marilyn Kielbasa, *Believing in a Media Culture* (Winona, MN: Saint Mary's Press, 1996), 38, diagram adapted.

26. Maurice Cranston, "ideology," *Encyclopedia Britannica*, last updated February 22, 2024, https://www.britannica.com/topic/ideology-society.

27. Suzanne Wilson, "ASU Professor says technology adding dimensionality to digital communication," *ASU News*, February 8, 2022, https://news.asu.edu/20220208-discoveries-online-dating-booming-changing-pandemic-era.

28. Stacy Jo Dixon, "Online dating worldwide—Statistics and Facts," *Statista* (website), published December 18, 2023, https://www.statista.com/topics/7443/online-dating/#topicOverview.

29. James Alberione, *Notes in Pastoral Theology*, trans. Andres R. Arboleda, Jr. (Rome: Edizioni San Paolo, 2001), 344.

30. Alberione, *Thoughts*, 170.

31. Nancy Usselmann, FSP, *A Sacred Look: Becoming Cultural Mystics* (Eugene, OR: Cascade Books, 2018), xxv.

32. Alberione, *Ut Perfectus Sit Homo Dei*, 455.

33. Forest Whitaker, interviewed by Alexandra Owens, "5 Questions with Forest Whitaker," November 30, 2016, https://www.sothebys.com/en/articles/5-questions-with-forest-whitaker.

34. Pope Francis, "Vigil with Young People, Address of His Holiness," January 26, 2019, https://www.vatican.va/content/francesco/en/speeches/2019/january/documents/papa-francesco_20190126_panama-veglia-giovani.html.

35. Alberione, *Thoughts*, 167.

36. James Alberione, *A Year with Ven. James Alberione*, ed. J. Maurus (Bombay: St Pauls, 2000), 103.

37. "Seven Themes of Catholic Social Teaching," United States Conference of Catholic Bishops, accessed February 12, 2024, https://www.usccb.org/beliefs-and-teachings/what-we-believe/catholic-social-teaching/seven-themes-of-catholic-social-teaching.

38. Paul VI, "If you want peace, work for justice," January 1, 1972, https://www.vatican.va/content/paul-vi/en/messages/peace/documents/hf_p-vi_mes_19711208_v-world-day-for-peace.html.

39. Paul VI, "If you want peace, work for justice."

40. "Video Game Market Size, Share & Trends Analysis Report By Device (Console, Mobile, Computer), By Type (Online, Offline), By Region (Asia Pacific, North America, Europe), And Segment Forecasts, 2023 – 2030," Grand View Research, accessed February 12, 2024, https://www.grandviewresearch.com/industry-analysis/video-game-market.

41. Greg Young, interviewed by Anna McAllister, "Fort Lauderdale barber cuts hair while also working to help those in need," April 23, 2023, https://www.cbsnews.com/miami/news/fort-lauderdale-barber-cuts-hair-while-also-working-to-help-those-in-need/.

42. Aelred of Rievaulx, *Spiritual Friendship* Book Two, trans. Lawrence C. Braceland (Collegeville, MN: Liturgical Press, 2010), 92.

43. *The Lord of the Rings: The Return of the King*, directed by Peter Jackson (Burbank, CA: New Line Cinema, 2003) DVD.

44. Alberione, *Thoughts*, 33–34.

45. Alberione, *Thoughts*, 160.

46. Antonia Salzano Acutis, *My Son Carlo: Carlo Acutis Through the Eyes of His Mother*, with Paolo Rodari (Huntington, IN: Our Sunday Visitor Publishing, 2023), 231.

47. Acutis, *My Son Carlo*, 231.

48. Booker T. Washington, *The Story of My Life and Work* (Naperville: J. L. Nichols & Co., 1900), 277, https://babel.hathitrust.org/cgi/pt?id=emu.010001059263&seq=5.

49. ABC News GMA, "This teen's struggle with depression led her and brother to create app to help others," February 2, 2018, https://abcnews.go.com/GMA/Wellness/teens-struggle-depression-led-brother-create-app/story?id=52791054#:~:text=The%20notOK%20app%20was%20created,a%20development%20company%20in%20Savannah.

50. Nicki Lisa Cole, Ph.D, "Definition of Consumerist Culture," ThoughtCo., November 6, 2019, thoughtco.com/consumerist-culture-3026120.

51. Skye Jethani, *The Divine Commodity* (Grand Rapids, MI: Zondervan, 2009), 110.

52. Sister Clare's Personal Writings, https://www.sisterclare.com/en/her-life/writings/personal/8500-sister-clare-s-devotion-to-the-eucharist.

53. Alberione, *Thoughts*, 38.

54. Alberione, *Thoughts*, 40.

55. Pope Francis (@pontifex), Twitter, April 28, 2013.

56. Megan Hull, ed., "Internet Addiction Facts and Statistics," August 02, 2022, https://www.therecoveryvillage.com/process-addiction/internet-addiction/internet-addiction-statistics/.

57. Keith W Beard and Eve M Wolf, "Modification in the Proposed Diagnostic Criteria for Internet Addiction," CyberPsychology & Behavior, June 2001, https://doi.org/10.1089/109493101300210286.

58. Petros Levounis, MD, M.A. and James Sherer, MD, eds., *Technological Addictions* (Washington, DC: American Psychiatric Association Publishing, 2022), 8.

59. Phil Longstreet and Stoney Brooks, "Life satisfaction: a key to managing internet and social media addiction," Technology in Society, May 28, 2017, 73–74, http://dx.doi.org/10.1016/j.techsoc.2017.05.003.

60. Adapted from Internet and Technology Addicts Anonymous, https://internetaddictsanonymous.org/.

61. John Paul II, *Man and Woman He Created Them*, 185–86.

62. John Paul II, *Man and Woman He Created Them*, 364–78.

63. Marcel LeJeune, *Cleansed: A Catholic Guide to Freedom from Porn* (Boston, MA: Pauline Books & Media, 2016), 23.

64. Samuel L. Perry and Cyrus Schleifer, "Till Porn Do Us Part? A Longitudinal Examination of Pornography Use and Divorce," The Journal of Sex Research, 55(3), 284–96, 2018, https://doi.org/10.1080/00224499.2017.1317709.

65. Gary Wilson, *Your Brain on Porn: Internet Pornography and the Emerging Science of Addiction* (UK: Commonwealth Publishing, 2017), 14–15.

66. Wilson, *Your Brain on Porn*, 22.

67. Todd Love, Christian Laier, Matthias Brand, Linda Hatch, and Raju Hajela. 2015. "Neuroscience of Internet Pornography Addiction: A Review and Update." Behavioral Sciences 5:388–433. doi: 10.3390/bs5030388. Crossref. PubMed.

68. See *Catechism of the Catholic Church*, no. 2352, 2354.

69. LeJeune, *Cleansed*, 107.

70. *Catechism of the Catholic Church*, no. 2339.

Pauline
BOOKS & MEDIA

A mission of the Daughters of St. Paul

As apostles of Jesus Christ,
evangelizing today's world:

We are CALLED to holiness
by God's living Word and Eucharist.

We COMMUNICATE the Gospel message
through our lives and through all
available forms of media.

We SERVE the Church
by responding to the hopes and needs
of all people with the Word of God,
in the spirit of St. Paul.

For more information visit us at:
www.pauline.org